HOW TO REACH YOUR LIFE GOALS

Keys To Help You Fulfill Your Dreams

D1270520

HOW TO REACH YOUR LIFE GOALS

Keys To Help You Fulfill Your Dreams

by
*Pete*r J. Daniels

Tulsa, Oklahoma

How To Reach Your Life Goals — Keys To Help You Fulfill Your Dreams
ISBN 1-56292-088-X
Copyright © 1995 by Peter J. Daniels
World Centre for Entrepreneurial Studies
38-40 Carrington Street
Adelaide, South Australia 5000
AUSTRALIA

Published by Honor Books
P.O. Box 55388
Tulsa, Oklahoma 74155

Dedicated to my friend,
Paul J. Meyer,
the world's master
goal-setter.

GOALS

If you are uncertain, timid or vague,

If you are not sure which is the way.

If you are concerned what the future will bring,

If you are dissatisfied with any old thing.

If you are fearful of what tomorrow may be,

If you are willing to forever be free.

Then you need to take hold of your life from this day,

And you must plan a far better way.

It's goals that you need to straighten you out,

To smooth out the paths and to get you about.

For goals set a sight that is clear and is bright,

And goals give you purpose to strive and to fight.

Your life is of value and the world is your home,

So stop now and think of where you should roam.

Just make a new start, to win and to claim,

A fresh firm new goal with a definite aim.

Then chase after your goal with a desperate desire,

With passion and excellence, as if you were on fire.

Do not be timid or reluctant or slow,

Just move into top gear and let all systems go.

Peter J. Daniels

CONTENTS

CONTENTS

FOREWORD

I'm extremely proud, honored, and complimented, to be given an opportunity to compose a foreword to one of the best books ever written on "goal setting."

How To Reach Your Life Goals is written by my friend of many years — Peter Daniels. He's a charter member of the International Board of Directors of the Crystal Cathedral Ministries. He has provided visionary leadership for our TV ministry in Australia where he is a very distinguished citizen.

The first time I read *How To Reach Your Life Goals*, I learned more than I have learned from any other single source on the principles, the power, and the possibilities in setting personal goals!

Read it. You'll gain insights and expand your awareness of the exciting goal setting business — more than you've ever known before in your life.

No one could read this book without having a growth experience in the most important department of a lifetime: *To set goals and let them lift you!*

Congratulations! You have opened the door to a genuine growth experience that I promise will be fantastic!!

Dr. Robert Schuller

ACKNOWLEDGEMENTS

The author would like to
give special thanks to
Peter and Erica Haran
for their valued assistance
in the writing of this book.
Excellence is their style.

INTRODUCTION

This book is not a collection of other people's writings or ideas. It did not come from a desire to write or a feeling or knowledge. It is not from the high scaffolds of academia, nor is it based on ignorance. But it does come from more than a quarter-century of failures, successes, frustrations, disappointments, exhilaration, obstacles, sweat, sleepless nights and a desperate desire to achieve!

The possible difference between this book and others is that I have tried and tested every item and principle suggested. I warn you not to expect a miracle by reading this book; a miracle already has been performed by your existence. But you can fulfil a miracle by making the principles you are prepared to adopt a part of your life.

I have lectured on the subject "How To Reach Your Life Goals" around the world at the request of others. This book results from a call for additional information.

You will discover early in the book a very strange element which is rarely discussed in other books on motivation. That is, success presupposes the willingness to bear pain. In understanding the implication of that principle, you may identify with some of the words first written by a successful man — Paul, the apostle, who said: "I pommel my body into submission." (1 Cor. 9:27 RSV, paraphrased.)

I hope you find within these pages the spark to light your flame. I expect — even hope — that many will improve on what I have written. I have avoided wasting words on embellishment. So brevity, not verbosity, will mark these pages.

Finally, I hope I achieve my goals in writing this book by turning you, the reader, into a motivated achiever.

CHAPTER ONE

PREPARING FOR LIFE GOALS

THE DESIRE

The very fact that you are reading this book indicates that you have a desire to achieve your life goals. You exchanged your money for a purpose, and you expect to realize that purpose.

This is basically true of all human actions. They are based on a desire either to gain an advantage or to avoid a disadvantage. The action of hurting or maiming another human being, for example, is normally preceded by a desire for revenge, or supremacy, or protection or gain. Even if a person says that he did something just because he felt like it, the desire to do it was triggered from the deep recesses of his mind. The desire accelerated the action.

Similarly, when you or I do something we really don't want to do, we are satisfying a desire which has probably become a habit in our life. Perhaps we are trying to avoid the consequences of something else that we are not prepared to cope with — and thus want to do even less!

It takes a certain amount of mind-sifting to identify desires and to face up to the realities of the motives that stimulate them. The best way to understand desires is to creep up on them gently, as it were. Whatever you do, don't try to meet them head on. Otherwise, you may trigger subconscious shock waves which just push them in even deeper and make the task of identifying them even more difficult — perhaps impossible. What you should do is casually ask yourself this question: How far would I be prepared to go to achieve (or avoid) this goal? Do not score a plus or minus sign against your answer, because all you are trying to establish at this stage is identification, not evaluation. If you experiment like this for a few weeks and just enjoy discovering the true depth of your desires, after a while your motives will become readily apparent.

Take care to examine your desires for false signals that may indicate hereditary or parochial habit patterns which have no real meaning to you as an individual. Simplify your desire profile by removing items and habits that are not really a part of you. Experience the simplicity of removing all the unwanted and heavy baggage that belongs to another time, or another person or another place.

In creating your own value system, remember that there must be some pride in who you are and what you stand for. A cleansing at this point may prevent false starts, doubts and failures later on. You need to recognize your present desire base and keep your options open for growth within your value system. (We will deal more with this subject later.) In setting goals for life, there are many checkpoints for discovery which will influence you, both in highlighting and expanding them.

The next step, of course, is to dig deeper, remove the desire curtain and look for basic motives. The essential skill here is to be transparently honest. We humans are so programmed from birth to perform to other people's expectations or codes of conduct, that you may need to ask the question, Where do my desires really come from?

A good measure to use in examining true motives is to ask yourself this question: *What proportion of my life am I prepared to give in exchange for accomplishing this desire?* In other words, Do my desires reflect just what I would *like* to have happen, or what I am *prepared to sacrifice* to have happen?

The third step is to draw up a mini-plan based on your past integrity and your past performance with respect to both the motives behind your actions — and the things you do to protect your motives.

The questions that need to be asked here are:

1. Am I always consistent in my main mode of expression?

2. Do I use motives out of context?

3. Have my motives changed unknowingly over the years from previously set positions?

Your answers to these questions will help you assess the stability of your motives and thereby appreciate the consistency of your desire.

Desire is the emotional thrust resulting from strong compulsive motives. So the clearer the motive, the stronger the desire.

It is of paramount importance to have clarity of thought at the motive level. This very often leads to a position of challenge with respect to how a real and believable value system is assessed. It is at this level that I believe the Christian Gospel with its absolute principles provides me with the strong, deep, believable motives that give root to my desire to strive and to achieve within the boundaries with which I feel inwardly at peace.

THE WILL

In my opinion, the will is the integrity of the soul.

Many people who experience difficulty in exercising their willpower never get past the gritting-of-the-teeth stage. They become discouraged because of the continual failure of their willpower. As the word itself suggests, willpower is putting power into the will from the desires created by interior motives. Therefore, a strong, chain effect is exhibited rather than a single decision of the will. Integrity is paramount in developing willpower. Without this honesty factor, energy is dissipated and confusion is likely to prevail.

One of the reasons we have difficulty in keeping our personal commitments is because they are just that — personal. We often override a personal commitment in a way we would rarely do with a commitment made to someone else. The key here is transparency with integrity. It is something akin to an oath of allegiance made to our self. Very often the strength of commitment to the will goes hand in hand with self-esteem and self-love. You and I would have great difficulty in respecting anyone who continually broke commitments to us. Likewise we will not respect our own inner integrity if we break our commitments to our own self.

I can remember someone asking me once if I had a program to keep fit. I replied, "I get up every workday morning and run."

"What if it is raining?" I was asked, "or, if it is very hot?"

"I have made a commitment to myself," I replied, "to exercise regularly until my eighty-fifth birthday. To ask myself every morning whether the weather is suitable for me to exercise would be a lack of confidence in my integrity to fulfil that to which I have committed myself."

We can very often do more by committing less by simply completing that which we have willed to do!

There are some simple observations which will shed light on dark areas in the mystique of willpower. Punctuality and willpower tend to go hand in hand, for instance. So do tidiness and willpower. A positive mental attitude and a strong will generally appear to be partners in life. Of course, the opposites also tend to apply.

The reason I use these simple examples is to emphasize that you can very often strengthen your willpower by approaching it from another angle, such as punctuality (a respect for time), or tidiness (a respect for order) or a positive mental attitude (a respect for the mind).

Other similarities may come to mind which, if you work at them, could strengthen your resolve in other areas of life. The trick is to approach the situation from a different angle which allows for an easing into a new routine. I call this the "side-door method." In other words, instead of trying to increase your willpower in a general sort of way, tackle one issue at a time, preferably a less difficult one. What you will find is that success in the less difficult area will help you to succeed in the other. Such habit patterns tend to strengthen personal integrity and hence the will.

For instance, I once knew a man who had two problems. First of all, he was very much overweight. Second, he was always late. He didn't seem able to overcome either obstacle. However, he began to work on the punctuality problem. He found that when he had managed to overcome this bad habit and was able to keep appointments on time, he also began to overcome his weight problem as well.

To play games with yourself at this stage is to put down weak foundations, and the test of time will always reveal weaknesses. When the winds of life blow hard, integrity will stand, but weak structures will fall.

POINTERS

➤ 1. ACCEPT THAT AN ACT OF WILL IS AN ACT OF INTEGRITY.

➤ 2. THE WILL CAN BE STRENGTHENED BY USING THE SIDE DOOR METHOD.

➤ 3. A DECISION TO ACT IS MADE ONCE, AND VACILLATION ONLY BREEDS WEAKNESS OF WILL.

THE PRICE

There is a price to pay for success. In most cases, the exchange rate for establishing commitment will depend on requirements. It will not necessarily be total. In fact, since each individual is different in so many complex ways, it will vary from person to person. But some principles do apply.

First, the cost will probably continue on a life-time basis. We, and the portion of our self that we are prepared to trade with, form the basis of the exchange. This, of course, is not a new thought. Well we remember that Satan tried to trade with Jesus at the top of a high mountain. The spiritual commitment of the Savior for the redemption of mankind far outshone the shallowness of the suggested deal.

Second, the price for commitment is a living thing, not a dead thing, such as money. Just by living, we are subject to variations of mood and complexities of circumstances. That is why our trade is often varied. We pay more or less for our commitment and integrity today than we paid yesterday, or will pay tomorrow. But pay we must. There are no bad debts to be transferred. If we pay up, we win; if we avoid payment, we lose. It's as simple as that. The cost is always the same in principle — an exchange of one section of life for another.

Third, the bargain is binding but fair. What we exchange for our commitment-integrity is often frustration, failure, disappointment and fear. What we often receive in return is confidence, success, optimism and courage.

You may be told from time to time by others that you are on the losing side. At those times you need only to reaffirm in your mind your value system as a checkpoint. It is possible to get off track, so establish a pattern of affirmation to keep your objectives clear. (We will deal more with affirmation later.)

Price is the acid test of sovereignty over the will. It must establish a return greater than the original cost. This fact must continually activate the will and strengthen the desire when the mind and body tire, and doubt creeps in. An interesting thing about paying the price for a personal pre-determined desire is that the price is virtually fixed, because control is being exercised.

Conversely, if cost is left to the elements of life, it will change like the state of one's digestion!

Of course, you will experience discomfort at times, and the price may seem exorbitant when compared with the immediate returns. But the long-term view must always occupy your focus. You must never contemplate immediate, cheap merchandise that is ill-suited and short-lived.

In fact, when you have not made up your mind about the price you are prepared to pay in terms of time, effort and self-sacrifice, you will find yourself on the defensive and trying to avoid the pain level of a disciplined will. Moreover, you will expose yourself to the attacks of others, not to mention factors like a prevailing economic climate, changing standards and so on.

The Bible speaks of renewing the mind as protection against changing times. (Rom. 12:2.) Within that thought is a control factor given by God to every human being. It is up to each of us to grasp it and use it wisely.

CHAPTER TWO

ASSESSING YOUR POSITION

"Positioning" is a relatively new word, but its implications have been around since the beginning of human existence. Positioning can be a matter of accident, of simply being in the right place at the right time. It has to do with timing, location, markets, the economy, world events, shortages and gluts. It has no particular sign or label, but its fruit abounds almost everywhere and almost all of the time. Just as a soccer match has sections of the field in full flight a large percentage of the time, so does life — and the ball usually goes to the best-positioned player.

You can position yourself by studying trends and markets and generally recognizing hidden opportunities.

Good positioning comes from learning and applying three simple rules:

1. *Make sure you are the initiator.*

This does not mean that you always have to be first, but it does mean that you should recognize that somewhere in the cycle of events a unique opportunity exists in which you can provide a service or alleviate a problem. The key is to recognize change, or pending change, and shift yourself accordingly to act as a pivot point. Set this task as a life pattern so that your goals can be reached by using your position.

2. *Maintain control in every situation.*

You are most of all responsible to yourself. To neglect that responsibility will finally render you impotent to assist your fellow man. Often we lose control through the fear of missing out on an opportunity, and on other occasions we may lose control when a situation becomes desperate and the axe is about to fall. Control is essential because it enables us to take advantage of a crisis rather than be disadvantaged by it.

3. *Do not be greedy.*

I have seen more people fail to succeed, or suddenly crash after succeeding, through greed than through any other factor in life. There is a quick way to measure your greed factor. Simply ask yourself the question: If I sold out now, would there be anything left for anyone else? You should be able to answer yes. Make a point of always leaving something for someone else if you have done well in a project. Remember, the person you think you do not need today often becomes the essential ally of tomorrow.

The final point to remember about personal positioning is this: In this shifting world keep placing yourself in the corner in which you want to operate. Avoid suspicion and excessive caution — such traits can paralyze you with fear and doubt. I believe that God placed us here on this earth in a fixed position of time and space. It was no mistake. Our unique situation is full of possibilities, so we should follow through and adopt the perfect position to achieve our life goals.

POINTERS

➤ 1. MAKE SURE YOU ARE THE INITIATOR.

➤ 2. MAINTAIN CONTROL IN EVERY SITUATION.

➤ 3. DO NOT BE GREEDY.

FAMILY POSITIONING

The family into which a person is born is possibly one of the most important positioning aspects of his life. There are the fortunate ones born into wealth, prestige and power. The less fortunate are born into poverty or a traumatic family environment.

My own background provided definite limitations, but as I became older I learned that the family I was to develop, with my own wife and children, was far more important, and therefore far more influential in my family positioning, than I could ever have imagined.

You can create, under the hand of God, the kind of family environment you want and are prepared to pay the price to have. This decision will reflect your own values and aspirations, which will exert an affirming effect on your positioning, as well as provide a family positioning springboard for your children.

I am not talking here about social status as much as ethical and attitudinal status. If you maintain a high ethical standard in your family, then everyone in the family wins, along with the community as a whole. A great deal of my early career was spent "unlearning" attitudes and ethics which were holding me back. Likewise, most of the time I spend counseling others today relates to locked-in ethical and attitudinal behavior traits that need to be dismantled and replaced before success can be obtained.

SOCIAL POSITIONING

In my opinion, social positioning is a choice. Provided respect and honesty prevail, one stratum of society is no better than the other. You can be super-successful on any level, but you are wise to select where you are going to be most comfortable in relation to your desires and personality. Be prepared to make changes if necessary. The key is maneuverability. Develop the ability to fit into any level and to accept people where they are and how they are. As you do so, watch your positioning expand its boundaries and widen opportunities for yourself. Remember, you can change your position temporarily or permanently. You only have to work at it and give it time.

A study of etiquette will allow you the freedom of knowing the right thing to do and will give you the confidence required for most situations.

Another factor to be considered is the fact that social positioning also limits and locks in one's influence. Developing and maintaining a well-rounded social structure is of more benefit than staying with one executive group and thus not benefiting from exposure and opportunities at different levels. Someone once said, "Be nice to people on your way up — you will meet the same people on the way down!"

POSITIONING BY EXPERIENCE

Much of what you and I are today is a result of past experience. This situation can often lead to a claustrophobic feeling — a sense that we are somehow "locked in" into an unchangeable position. This is simply not true — experience is in the past, and it can stay there. *I contend that it is never too late to change.* The secret to making use of past experience is selectivity.

Do this: Examine carefully and objectively the effects upon you of past experiences — the good and the bad, recent or distant. Write them down and study them.

Generally you will find that past experiences have a suppressive effect and act as danger signals to prevent painful recurrences. It is the bad experiences that are locked away — consciously or subconsciously — and which often cause failure in life as those unpleasant memories are allowed to linger on. It is necessary at this stage to take a closer look at the subconscious, which includes the imagination, if you are going to become a goal-setter.

The subconscious is one of three things: 1) a powerful ally under control, 2) a machine left in neutral or 3) an enemy out of control, regurgitating bad experiences. If you are serious about improving your performance and quality of life, it will be essential that you make a continued effort to identify problem areas of past experience. Separate out fact from fiction, replay past events in your mind and seek the benefits from each event. Then program the good and dispense with the bad.

Any business that is worth its salt has a company policy based on good and bad experience input. Develop your own personal policy for growth by developing clear guidelines of attitude and behavior based on past experience. Document both the things that you know have helped you in the past and the things that you need to avoid because they have caused you anguish. Remember to look for good always, because your imagination will usually pick up the disaster areas, and your subconscious will readily absorb them as real experience — which will influence your future output.

POINTERS

➤ 1. YOU CAN CREATE UNDER THE HAND OF GOD THE KIND OF ENVIRONMENT YOU ARE PREPARED TO PAY THE PRICE TO HAVE.

➤ 2. DEVELOP THE ABILITY TO ACCEPT PEOPLE WHERE THEY ARE AND HOW THEY ARE.

➤ 3. THE SECRET OF MAKING USE OF PAST EXPERIENCE IS SELECTIVITY.

POSITIONING BY EDUCATION

Who among us has not felt the limiting factors of education? The more we learn, the more we realize there is to learn. The real question each of us needs to ask our self is, Do I understand the simple principles of life and comprehend its flow?

I am forever receiving letters of request from mediocre performers for updated information on new and highly specialized psychological and learning advances. In our modern society, there appears to be a misguided notion that "the more advanced information I can collect, the more successful I will become." Educators in general have encouraged this ill-founded and unproven philosophy to the point that an army of "information gatherers" has developed.

Look into the life of your nearest friend or acquaintance who is successful, and you will discover that, whether schooled or unschooled, he uses the education he has to the fullest extent and continues to build upon that education in line with present and future goals. But rarely does such a person gather information that is neither practical nor useful.

Education is expandable and changeable and should be adaptable.

It is useless to set goals in one direction and then to waste valuable time and energy expanding knowledge in some other area. Assess where you are now as far as your education is concerned, and then evaluate what you need to know to get where you want to go. Set your sights on acquiring information as a tool to get the job done.

POINTERS

➤ 1. DON'T BE A WASTEFUL "INFORMATION GATHERER."

➤ 2. REMEMBER, YOU CAN CHANGE YOUR EDUCATION DIRECTION.

➤ 3. ALWAYS SEEK TO EXPAND YOUR EDUCATION IN LINE WITH THE WAY YOU ARE GOING.

➤ 4. SEEK OUT PRACTICAL INFORMATION RELATING TO YOUR NEEDS.

SUCCESS

In assessing your present position, be fair with yourself, particularly in regard to past successes. Nobody has failed at everything. Everyone has experienced at least some successes in life. Those successes you have enjoyed in your past can be used as building blocks. Count them up and evaluate how you won the day. Was it luck, timing, special knowledge, hard work, risk or relevant information? Now write it down; log those things you have done well and be generous with yourself.

As a success-oriented person, remember that *success is not a dirty word*. Although it is mentioned only one time in the *King James Version* of the Bible, (Josh. 1:8), it is encouraged throughout Scripture in the form of the words "prosper" and "prosperity." (1 Chron. 22:13; 2 Chron. 20:20; Ps. 1:3; 35:27; 1 John 2.) Keep in mind too that mankind was created to subdue the earth and exercise dominion over it (Gen. 1:27,28), which gives us human beings a sovereign charter for growth and achievement with no room for contemplation of failure.

Success is for you because humanity itself strives always to win, to obtain, to overcome and to possess. Every new-born baby is evidence of that hope and promise. Every new step taken by a young child illustrates success and accelerates the youngster on to greater achievement.

Success is for you because God committed it to your development within the confines of the biblical charter. You were created, programmed and given opportunities to succeed, and the responsibility to do so is now yours. Becoming a success involves assuming full responsibility in the areas of:

1. *planning*

2. *development*

3. *achievement*

4. *failure*

5. *behavior*

31

The proper handling of this responsibility demonstrates a personal growth, a commitment to others and a respect for truth, which will lead to the fulfillment of ultimate potential.

FAILURE

At one time or another we have all felt the helplessness of despair and failure. An old-timer once said, "You don't learn anything from the second kick of a horse." This ought to be true, of course, but for most of us it takes three or four kicks before things start to sink in!

I remember my first business failure. After the humility and disappointment, I was feeling very sorry for myself, but I soon came to the unmistakable conclusion that the fault lay directly within me. The evidence for this conclusion was quite clear! Other people were running similar businesses with similar restraints and difficulties, but they were successful. It was painful to accept the hard, cold fact that my frivolous attitude toward money was the real problem.

The second time I went broke was because of my sloppy attitude about keeping proper records and my negligence in clarifying one step before moving on to the next.

The third time I failed was because I was chasing a dream without taking steps to avoid the twin nightmares of over-estimating my own ability and leaning too much upon other people.

Out of all such experiences, lessons can be learned. Assess your present position and provide the foundation for setting your goals. Don't overlook the lessons learned from failures, and certainly do something to rectify weaknesses, but *always keep your eye on the lesson learned, not on the destructiveness of failure.*

And learning lessons is what failure is — or should be — all about.

During one five-year period in my business life, it seemed that I could not do anything right. My wife said, "Give up and go to work for someone else."

"Never!" I said. "God knows what a stubborn fool I am, and He's teaching me a lesson."

From this experience I discovered an important principle: *If you keep making the same mistakes, you will never graduate, because you have not learned your lessons properly.* It's as simple as that. If you do make the same mistake twice, examine it in close detail, learn a lesson from it and don't forget it.

Another point worth noting is: *Don't break well-learned principles.* You do so at your peril, as my son Graham once found out. He lost an enormous amount of money and after eighteen months of struggle I asked him what lessons he had learned from the experience. He said, "In the future I will maintain control."

Control is a vital life principle.

POINTERS

➤ 1. DON'T LET FAILURES CRUSH YOU - REMEMBER, FAILURES ARE LESSONS.

➤ 2. EXPERIENCING THE SAME FAILURE TWICE RARELY TEACHES YOU ANYTHING NEW; IT JUST EMPHASIZES THE LESSON.

➤ 3. DOCUMENT YOUR LESSONS INTO LIFE-PRINCIPLES TO PREVENT THEIR RECURRENCE.

➤ 4. OVERCOMING FAILURE BUILDS CHARACTER AND IS A LADDER TO SUCCESS.

➤ 5. **FAILING IN LIFE IS LIKE FAILING IN SCHOOL — YOU DON'T MOVE UP TO THE NEXT GRADE UNTIL YOU HAVE LEARNED YOUR LESSONS IN THIS ONE.**

EXPOSURE

Exposure is important because it produces experience, and with experience comes valuable knowledge. Timid minds never venture into the world of exposure. However, timidity can be overcome by mentally accepting the fact that the results of "the worst that can happen" can often serve as the instigating force to make sure that it never happens again.

Remember — nothing is as final as it seems at the time.

Businesses can be rebuilt, broken bodies can be healed. Even damaged or destroyed reputations can be resurrected, and financial security can be regained. There is an abundance of evidence in every city or town of someone who has overcome simply by being prepared to enter into the arena one more time. This means, of course, more exposure, more risk, more experience and thankfully more knowledge.

Avoiding exposure is like trying to become proficient at riding a bicycle without getting on it! You have to mount it and have a few falls and near misses to become accomplished at riding it. So is the principle of life's progress. Sometimes you have to expose yourself to danger, failure, embarrassment and ridicule in order to achieve security, success, confidence and esteem.

I am not suggesting that you ignore sound advice, but I am urging you to be bold in exposure, so that in the future you may have the recall to form informed opinions, develop confidence and apply the principles you have learned from personal experience.

Particularly try to seek exposure in situations in which you can gain valuable experience at little or no cost to yourself. Gain exposure by accepting an official position in your club; by so doing, you will gain experience dealing with people. Help with the finance campaigns for your church or charity or the political party of your choice. Offer to debate subjects or volunteer to help with community projects. Take on an extra risk at work and stay a little later to become proficient at something new. Try a new sport. Go camping in the wilderness. Learn to water-ski or ride a horse. Acquire an agency or a franchise for a saleable product and learn to market it, or make something to sell. Confront a person who has been bullying or harassing you. Build your exposure ratio as another foundation stone toward your support system for accomplishing your life goals.

POINTERS

> 1. IF YOU ARE WITHOUT EXPOSURE, YOU ARE WITHOUT EXPERIENCE.

> 2. GAIN EXPOSURE AND YOU GAIN INEXPENSIVE EXPERIENCE.

> 3. CONFRONT SITUATIONS IN ORDER TO STRENGTHEN RESOLUTIONS.

CHAPTER THREE

RECOGNIZING YOUR PERSONALITY STRENGTHS

THE PEOPLE PERSON

In preparing your life goals, try looking much deeper into yourself as a person than you are now doing. Analyze your personality, because self-knowledge is essential in programming a life. Stand back and take a good look at yourself. Accept that a personality can, in fact, be developed in various areas to suit goal needs.

Take first *the people person.* He is the one who loves to gather with people; he immensely enjoys the company of others. He is easily recognized at any get-together. His gregarious nature and friendly behavior are plain to see as he moves from one group to the next. Generally, he is the first to arrive and the last to leave. When he does finally depart, he has usually made arrangements to get together again or to meet with someone at a later date.

The people person, you'll find, is the one who remembers names, recalls past events and rehearses previous meetings. This is because he is intensely interested in people and is well-liked by others.

I am not a people person. To this day I would be perfectly content living in total isolation — thinking, reading, writing and enjoying my own company. But I had to change my personality to become more gregarious, develop better conversational skills and get along more easily with other people. I had to do so quite simply because it was part of achieving my life goals.

Goal-setters are people persons due to a God-given principle — we human beings were not created to be isolationists. We are part of a giant family of mankind; we were put here to help one another.

So develop your people-person personality, which will allow you to move in any circle. As you become more sensitive and compassionate toward others, you will obtain the side effect of strengthening your own character.

POINTERS

➤ 1. GOAL-SETTERS CONDITION THEIR OWN LIFE.

➤ 2. GOAL-SETTERS CONDITION THE LIFE OF OTHERS.

➤ 3. GOAL-SETTERS REMAIN IN THE MAINSTREAM OF LIFE.

➤ 4. GOAL-SETTERS ACHIEVE THEIR LIFE GOALS.

THE BOOK PERSON

A *book person* is simply one who feels confident in the reliability of the written word. I am not talking about someone who simply finds entertainment in pleasure reading or who seeks to escape harsh reality through fiction. No, I am referring to the person who is fascinated and attracted by books that develop and inspire.

However, an important point to remember is that the writers of books are also human, with the same fears, failures and frustrations that are common to all of us. In real life, many authors would be a surprise to their readers. I have met some authors who expose their lives clearly and expound their views confidently on the printed page, but who wilt in private conversation or public debate.

On the other hand, there are some people who simply do not enjoy reading and who fail in discussion when confronted by someone with a deep knowledge of recorded facts.

I used to avoid reading with the usual excuses of lack of time, inability to concentrate and difficulty in comprehension. But then I discovered that the mind is like a muscle: do enough push-ups, and it will expand and absorb and become flexible. Surely, I reasoned, if I read enough and expanded my vocabulary, I would come to enjoy reading and would eventually reap the benefits. It still amazes me how true that observation is. My life has expanded through reading, more than I ever dreamed possible.

Make it a practice, if you are a book person, to be with people more often. Ask them questions about themselves, their families and interests; become more public and take a higher profile. Conversely, if you are not a book person, you must realize that you have cut yourself off from a valuable source of knowledge.

Both book persons and people persons can expand their horizons by reading applicable material and fellowshipping with other human beings.

POINTERS

➤ 1. DO NOT SUBSTITUTE BOOKS FOR PEOPLE.

➤ 2. YOU MAY KNOW IT IN THEORY, BUT DO YOU KNOW IT IN PRACTICE?

➤ 3. TUNE INTO OTHER PEOPLE'S EXPERIENCE.

➤ 4. YOU CAN BUILD READING AND CONCENTRATION SKILLS.

STYLE

Every one of us has style, that indefinable quality that gives us the stamp of individuality. It is very much an outward quality; we may be gruff, noisy, quiet, explosive or flamboyant. Style is what we do and the way we do it. What we are looking for here is a style that will help us achieve our life goals.

Let's look at some examples. If we are seeking to become the best undertaker in town, playing practical jokes on people will not be a recommended style. Similarly, drinking and eating in excess will not help us become a top athlete, if that is our life goal.

Have you ever met a famous person and said to yourself afterwards, "That's just how I imagined him to be?" Contrast that situation, if you will, with an occasion when you witnessed behavior from someone that was inconsistent with your image of him. Interesting, is it not?

I'm not talking here about showing off. I'm talking about shining on. I'm referring to the development of flair, style or presentation that puts a stamp on an individual and makes him stand out in a crowd.

A simple example came to me when I went to stay with some new friends in another state. When I entered the guest bedroom in their home I immediately noticed that they had hung a nicely colored, handwritten message on the wall which read, "Welcome, Peter Daniels, to our home." That was part of their style.

Exhibit your style when you entertain people, undertake a project, make a presentation to a group or introduce friends to other acquaintances.

When I appreciate something that people have done for me, I usually write a poem about them and then give it to them in person or mail it to them after the occasion. Can you imagine their response? How many people have ever had a poem written about them in their entire life? But that's my style.

When I travel overseas, I always take some Australian opals to give to people I meet. That's my style.

If I'm holding a dinner party, I make sure the doorman knows by name each of the guests who is coming, so they are greeted properly. That's my style.

If I commit myself to do something for someone else, I try to do a little more than is expected. That's my style.

If I'm going to promote anything, I make it a grand occasion. That's my style.

If I'm going to challenge something publicly, I make sure that my facts are startling and correct and, as a result, publicity automatically follows. That's my style.

What about you? Do you have a style that indicates success and provokes further growth? Recognizing your personality strengths and adding other strengths to them will enhance your life and increase your self-esteem. Seek to obtain a balance of the best characteristics of these three personality types:

* a people person

* a book person

* a person with style

Then use these characteristics to expand your usefulness and achieve your life goals.

POINTERS

➤ 1. YOU CAN EXPAND AND DEVELOP YOUR PERSONALITY.

➤ 2. DEVELOP A STYLE THAT IS CONSISTENT WITH WHO AND WHAT YOU ARE.

➤ 3. WRITE A DESCRIPTION OF THE STYLE YOU NEED TO DEVELOP AND FOLLOW IT.

PHYSICAL FITNESS

It has been said that a healthy body reflects a healthy mind. It could also be said that a healthy body can do whatever the healthy mind requires. Physical infirmity, however, reminds us of our total dependence upon God not only for our next step but even for our next breath.

Therefore, in setting your life goals, be sure to pay attention to your physical inabilities, whether hereditary or accidental. I well remember in my own life suffering from rheumatic fever, diphtheria, collapsed blood cells and meningitis. How vividly do I recall the difficulties I experienced during those dark days.

While we should not play up our infirmities, we should not ignore them either. Our goals should relate to our physical condition, especially if it is permanent. But regardless of our physical disability, it does not have to limit other possibilities. Paralysis may immobilize the body, but it does not have to immobilize the mind. A person who is physically immobile can use his brain to help him become a great composer, poet, inventor or stock market whiz. Infirmity in age is more of the mind than the body.

I am always amused at W. Clement Stone. When he comes to a business meeting, still in his nineties, he always greets people with the comment, "I feel happy, I feel healthy, I feel great, how about you?" Sir Bruce Small, a famous Gold Coast developer in Australia, inspired me many times, well after his eightieth birthday, when he would literally run up three flights of stairs to do business.

The key to overcoming or coming to grips with infirmity lies in the way it is related to with the mind.

Life is not just a body, it is also a mind and a spirit. Any physical position can either be overcome, or used as a pivot point, in attaining personal goals. If you are prone to be overweight, bring your eating under control. If you have a particular physical weakness, always seek out the best treatment that medical science can offer and avoid situations that will irritate the condition. But don't ever confuse physical weakness with mental weakness.

Some time ago, in our church, my wife and I were asked to pick up a lady who had recently had a minor operation on her feet. I escorted her to the car and during the ride to church she said that she didn't know how she would handle the compulsory voting in the upcoming federal elections.

"Why don't you phone the department?" I replied. "They will send you the appropriate forms to fill out."

After the church service, she again mentioned the matter, and I responded in the same way. She came back at me again, asking me if I would phone the appropriate department for her.

"No," I said. "Your problem is in your feet, nor in your head. You can easily do it yourself."

I remember that my wife was very concerned because she thought I had spoken too harshly. But there was no need for concern because the woman later told her: "Isn't your husband wonderful? That's what I needed — someone to talk to me like that."

We need to exercise our bodies daily, pay attention to the food we eat and monitor the amount of sleep we get. Performance and endurance — or lack of it — can often be directly traced to poor diet and fatigue. Take note at this point, however, that we should not expect a painless life or a physical high all the time. In addition, we all have our illnesses and accidents to contend with, and most of us have hereditary weaknesses with which we must cope. The trick is to recognize the ups and downs of everyday life, cope with them as they emerge and push ahead.

POINTERS

➤ 1. **RECOGNIZE PHYSICAL DEFECTS.**

➤ 2. **DO NOT AGGRAVATE THE DEFECT.**

➤ 3. **INCREASE YOUR PHYSICAL FITNESS WHERE POSSIBLE.**

➤ 4. **PUSH ON REGARDLESS OF HARDSHIPS, WEAKNESSES AND INFIRMITIES.**

CONCENTRATION

Concentration can be a frustrating part of life. So often we try to concentrate on the matter at hand only to find our minds drifting off and away.

I have often longed to be able to work by the sea or in a country retreat — a Shangri-la somewhere — with my wife at my side. I have learned the hard way that I am a loner; I can only concentrate in solitude, without noise or interruption. I have found the depth of my concentration at times to become so intense that when I am finished I am so exhausted I immediately fall asleep!

Deep concentration requires dedication, desperation and no interruptions.

Over the years I have learned to switch off from my surroundings when the time comes to wrestle with a problem or an idea. I know that if I don't complete the concentration circle, I will lose the connection and fail to produce what I want.

In many respects, concentration goes against our natural human nature and needs. Inwardly, we want to be at peace and enjoy release from pressure. Concentration disturbs both peace and release. And concentration often eludes us because we do not have a plan to reach what I call "the climax of concentration."

Try this method the next time you tackle a problem requiring ultimate concentration. First, formulate some heading that will require concentrated effort. Then find an atmosphere you know will be conducive to your commitment. Set aside a time frame big enough to create what I call the "flow." When concentrating, don't get into a sleep-type posture or make the mistake of thinking that you can develop concentration by thought drift. As you may know by now, concentration is hard work; if you do not accept that fact, you will disqualify yourself.

POINTERS

➤ 1. ACCEPT THE CHALLENGE OF CONCENTRATION.

➤ 2. **REALIZE THAT OTHERS HAVE TO OVERCOME IT ALSO.**

➤ 3. **PREPARE YOURSELF BY MAKING HEADLINES FOR CONCEN-TRATION.**

➤ 4. **FIND YOUR BEST CONCENTRATION LOCATION.**

➤ 5. **FORMULATE YOUR CONCENTRATION ON PAPER.**

PAIN ENDURANCE

In the introduction to this book I spoke of the willingness to bear pain in order to achieve success in a chosen life goal. The nature of man is to avoid pain, *yet pain at some level is often a strong component of goal achievement.*

Pain is a great teacher and a great preventer. The thought of pain can act as a preventative against action, while the discipline of pain can act as a motivator of action. Pain in its crudest form is a signal to do or not to do. But it can be much more. It is first of all a barrier that must be overcome. By passing through the pain barrier, it is possible to relish the euphoria that lies on the other side.

A friend of mine who does distance running tells me that in a long-distance race, when the pain is almost unbearable, he pushes on. As he does so, suddenly, as if by magic, the pain vanishes. A new sensation overwhelms him, and he is able to go on and finish the race.

The pain of failure blights all of us with a long, accusing finger, pointing with uncanny accuracy to our omissions and fractures. Yet we must press on and endure the pain, and even learn to accept it as a friend. We must learn to interpret those crude signals, though it may well be a painful experience. We will find out later in life that we had to endure pain in order to run the race and finish the course.

Pain in learning to succeed is one thing. It almost seems a badge of honor or a diploma placed on the wall of the hidden corridors in our private lives. Never think that the course is finished permanently, or that the so-called diploma is evidence of a lesson learned and a graduation completed.

Pain will be with you throughout your life, in success and in failure, in joy and in grief. It is the ever-present friend, enemy and trickster waiting in the shadows ready to pounce. It may be the pain you feel when a loved one makes a careless remark you know is not true, or a newspaper article represents you as someone you are not. It may be the fatigue you feel after an international flight when you are expected to perform at a speaking appointment in a manner worthy of a world professional — even when you are so tired you can hardly stand up.

Pain occurs when you have thoroughly prepared a project, dotted all the I's and crossed all the T's, only to discover that you have been let down and that the whole project has crumbled. Pain is the result of pressure being applied upon pressure. It occurs when your brain feels that it will burst it if retains one more fact or holds one more thought. Then there is the pain of having yet another person "open up" and "share" with you when you are already overshadowed and burdened down by other people's problems.

But it is endurance that counts. The trick is to break through the pain barrier to a full and overflowing life. There is a certain aura and weightlessness that is experienced when that barrier is broken. It is at these times that I identify with Paul the apostle when he says, "I pommel my body into submission." (1 Cor. 9:27 RSV, paraphrased.) In so doing, I understand the peace of God that surpasses our understanding. (Phil. 4:6,7 RSV).

POINTERS

> ➤ 1. **IN VARYING DEGREES PAIN IS GOING TO BE WITH YOU THROUGHOUT LIFE.**

> ➤ 2. **PAIN NEEDS TO BE IDENTIFIED AS A CRUDE SIGNAL THAT MAY NOT BE APPARENT TILL LATER.**

➤ 3. Beyond the pain threshold often awaits the prize.

SKILLS

To make a clear start on goal-setting, you must recognize your skills. Many skills are not apparent at first glance. However, on close examination it becomes obvious that every person has in-built skills.

Paying attention to detail may be one of your built-in skills. You may express yourself well verbally. You may be an excellent planner. You may handle people well or have the ability to do more than one thing at a time. Other skills may include having an inquiring mind, or being endowed with patience. All of these are inherent or developed and can be used in a positive way to achieve your life goals.

Some skills are locked away. They may appear at a time of crisis or great opportunity. You may have some skills that right now are being used at minimum capacity, while still others may be being totally neglected or misused.

Whatever your individual situation, you are uniquely equipped with obvious and hidden skills, learned and gifted endowments that need to be identified, developed and put to good use.

Years ago I used to call on a big store in a major country town to sell a product I was handling at the time. One day I received notice from the liquidator of this store explaining that the company was in financial difficulties and might have to close down. He indicated that they would continue for a few months to see how things worked out and that they would guarantee payments of all future goods received.

Later, a strange thing happened. Orders started to come in from the store again, but this time they were bigger than before. Naturally, I paid the company a visit only to find that the most insignificant department manager was now general manager and

CEO and was running the whole show. Evidently, he had convinced senior management that he could trade them out of their difficulties, and then had proceeded to exhibit skills that were not obvious before he saved the day. This man rose to full stature in a difficult situation. He had never before had the opportunity or been put under the pressure to exert himself — and thus to discover his latent skills.

You have skills, incredible skills. If you are the least bit serious about setting and reaching your life goals, you need to sharpen and document the skills that are obvious and dig deep and even put yourself into a stress situation in order to discover the hidden ones.

POINTERS

➤ 1. IDENTIFY YOUR PRESENT SKILLS.

➤ 2. PROVOKE YOURSELF INTO A SITUATION TO AWAKEN YOUR HIDDEN SKILLS.

➤ 3. CONTINUE TO DEVELOP NEW SKILLS.

CHAPTER FOUR

PUTTING YOUR LIFE TOGETHER

PUTTING YOURSELF TOGETHER
THE WAY YOU WOULD LIKE TO BE

If you had the magical power to change yourself into what you would really like to be, would you exercise that power? Of course you would. First, you would have to strip away the fantasy, and then you would have to get down to the nuts and bolts of what you would really want to make of yourself.

Most people, for a number of reasons, never get past the fantasy stage. Some are not aware that they really can make the change, while others are too lazy and self-indulgent even to try, preferring instead to throw up excuses and complaints as a defence so they can languish in comfort. After all, change requires effort.

So let's get serious for a moment and ask ourselves some hard questions, such as: What if I don't even like my appearance? I can't change that, right?

Wrong.

I faced a serious problem with protruding ears that was so acute I was nicknamed "saddle flaps." I came to the conclusion one day in my early forties that I was going to correct the problem. I

49

consulted a plastic surgeon and was greeted by a plethora of possibilities available through modern science. When I mentioned what I was going to do, a friend of mine told me it was vanity. I suggested that he take out his false teeth after every meal because that was all he needed them for — I have heard no more negative remarks from him! The results of the surgery were incredible, and the boost to my self-esteem was awesome.

You can change yourself physically in a variety of ways if you really want to, if you are serious and convinced that it will make a significant difference. The easiest way, of course, to change your appearance is with proper diet, exercise, posture, grooming and clothing. If you don't understand fashions suitable for your lifestyle, study them. Don't forget proper bearing; remember that the way you carry yourself makes an incredible difference.

Many years ago I was watching a television news broadcast, and I was suddenly arrested by the dress and deportment of a world leader. I then reflected on other world leaders and began to watch the way they were groomed.

I noticed that most international political figures dress the same way. Most Western leaders wear blue, grey or black suits (usually in that order of preference). Their well-tailored suits are accompanied by tasteful accessories, including conservative neckties, white shirts and black shoes, all immaculately coordinated. I made my mind up that was the way I wanted to look, and to this day you will never see me dressed in anything but those colors and styles.

Clothes may not make the man, but they certainly introduce him.

Now let's turn to the mind. Is your mind currently the way you want it to be? Believe it or not, you can change your mind, because God gave you a free will; He never "robotized" the mind of man. Develop habit force and change your mental attitude. Correct little faults. "Pull yourself up," in a manner of speaking, by your thinking habits and your attitude. The important thing to remember here is, never let an exception occur, because you will send messages to your subconscious that you are prepared to cheat.

Write down what sort of person you want to become. (It may seem that you need a magic wand — if that is the case, so be it.) Write down your goal in detail and include the physical, mental and personality traits you want to develop. And one more thing — include your spiritual self as well.

By now you may have realized that you do possess a powerful magic wand; it is called "choice," and it is waiting for you to press the button called "decision" to make the required adjustments in your life.

POINTERS

➤ 1. WORK OUT THE TYPE OF PERSON YOU WOULD REALLY LIKE TO BE.

➤ 2. IDENTIFY CLEARLY AND WRITE DOWN ON PAPER A FULL, DETAILED DESCRIPTION OF THAT PERSON.

➤ 3. ACTIVATE THE SWITCH CALLED "CHOICE" AND CREATE THAT PERSON IN YOU AND WITHIN YOU.

THE BELIEF FACTOR

The two largest stumbling blocks to a change in life are believability and mobility. The belief factor can usually be overcome by a convincing argument, peppered with facts and garnished with persuasion. Then attention can be turned to mobility, to getting on with the job. At that moment, the belief factor may again be called into question and a seesaw action may begin, absorbing time and energy but producing nothing.

If that is your experience at this stage, go back to the early chapters on desire, will and price, and clear away again the

51

accumulated debris of procrastination that prevents you from being honest with yourself and objective in your aim.

The libraries of the world are full of stories of enterprises with humble beginnings which expanded into giant corporations and business empires because supposedly insignificant people dared to believe and act. By so doing, they discovered that they could — and indeed actually did! — become great. These are stories of ordinary people, "underdogs" as it were, overcoming seemingly impossible odds, using limited means, and in the end triumphing in spite of obstacles and opposition.

You can be one of those people. You can do the impossible. You can expand your horizons. You can overcome. You can endure. You can achieve your life goals.

POINTERS

➤ 1. RECOGNIZE THE SEESAW BATTLE BETWEEN BELIEF AND MOBILITY AND PASS OVER ITS LIMITATIONS.

➤ 2. REREAD THE EARLIER CHAPTERS ON DESIRE, WILL AND PRICE.

➤ 3. INSPIRE YOURSELF WITH STORIES OF OTHER PEOPLE'S ACHIEVEMENTS AND ACCEPT THAT YOU CAN REACH YOUR OWN PERSONAL GOALS.

BEWARE OF THE CROWD

Now is the time to consider some warnings and mechanisms to protect against the insidiousness of "the crowd." Some great entrepreneurs claim that the crowd is almost always wrong. Find out, they say, which way the crowd is heading — then consider a different direction. It takes individual courage and commitment to assess what is right, and a crowd cannot do that; it can only confirm what is right. It has been said that man in the singular is unique and unpredictable, but that man in a group is easy to evaluate and predict.

Remember, you will be questioned by some about your newfound ambitions, goals or lifestyle. Never lose sight of the fact that those who question, criticize or oppose are normally part of the crowd.

The crowd rarely identifies itself as such. The people concerned may not even be acquainted with one another. But you will find that they clearly identify themselves by their remarks and posture.

The crowd can be devious in its actions. In the beginning, they will identify with you, even encourage you, rarely expecting you to raise your standard or achieve your goals (because they, too, had similar dreams and ambitions and in identifying with you they are stroking, as it were, their own desires).

But when you begin to demonstrate growth by producing results and adding wings to your dreams, the mood changes as the crowd sees the reflections of their failures in your successes; you become a yardstick to their lives and behavior. On the face of it, surface relationships are still intact, but be warned, there is an avalanche of criticism close at hand.

The picture becomes complete when you have achieved success. Now the crowd wants you as a friend; they are looking for the spin-off, and their attitudes become patronizing.

The stance I recommend adopting is not to put down the crowd, but to be aware of the destructive nature of their actions. Crowds can absorb energy and waste time. At times, we pay too much attention to what others think of us, how they react to our actions. Remain true to your value system and get on with the job. Jesus Christ, I am reminded, was welcomed into the city by the crowd, and it was the voice of the same crowd that later cried out, "Crucify Him!" (Mark 15:13.)

POINTERS

> 1. THE RESPONSIBILITY IS YOURS, NOT THE CROWD'S.

> 2. RECOGNIZE CHANGES IN THE CROWD, BUT DO NOT BE AFFECTED BY THEM.

> 3. YOUR LIFE IS YOUR OWN, CLAIM IT.

GOALS NEED FORM

If you were to ask any group of people, "What are goals?" you would get a number of answers — and a lot of confusion. I have tried it, and the lack of expression from some high achievers is amazing. It is not as though they are not using the goal-achieving process, their list of objectives substantiates that fact, but to pass that elusive quality on to others is quite another matter.

Goals are the solidification of dreams, ideas and ideals in practical form, for practical implementation, for practical completion. On the other hand, dreams are elusive and grand, and free from the restraints of the pragmatic. They form the seeds of inspiration that keep the hope machine in working order. Many goals are in the twilight zone of the imagination, like smoke from a fire, real but not "packageable." But if the source of that smoke is traced, it will lead to the flame that creates it.

Goals are the result of bringing dreams, ideas and ideals into tangible and "examinable" form.

Goals without the means to achieve them are only useful for flights of fancy, an occasional pick-me-up. Without a plan the goal may be evident, but something is missing; there is no bridge or mechanism to use to cross from fantasy to reality.

You must get your goals into written form; otherwise, you will continue to play mind games which belong in adolescence rather than adulthood. I say again, get the writing habit with thoughts, quotes, expressions and ideas. Plan your dream so that you can nail down your goals and the means to achieve them.

I see this as fencing off your dreams, goals, plans and means. When you write it all down, it cannot escape from your grasp and will not become fleeting, wasted moments.

I cannot stress enough the need to solidify your dreams with the written word and the need to do it quickly before the vapor of smoke vanishes and recall is lost.

POINTERS

➤ 1. **DREAMS ARE THE BIRTHPLACE OF GOALS.**

➤ 2. **WRITING DOWN GOALS ASSURES PERMANENCE.**

➤ 3. **ONLY SOLID GOALS CAN BE WORKED ON.**

GOALS NEED MAPS

"A goal must include a map."

I have often heard this statement, and there certainly is an element of truth in it. Maps provide information. They indicate prevailing conditions. They give direction.

Remember, life goals are identifiable but intangible. So you need a charted course to find the way. Your map to achieving your goals must be as explicit and clear as possible with as much detail packed in as you can manage.

Many a businessman has failed because he did not plan well. As the saying goes, "If you fail to plan, you plan to fail." Spend time visualizing a map and the form it should take, so it will remain a clear reminder of the task ahead.

I keep a small notation of my next ten years' goals in my wallet as a quick reference and ready reminder so I will not stray off course.

You need a life map to the end of your life simply because that is the intelligent thing to do. The good and the bad will come along, but you move the bias towards the good when you have planned and mapped out your future. If you still have some doubt about planning your life, remember that God takes it even farther — into eternity.

POINTERS

➤ 1. **CREATE A MAP TO REACH YOUR GOALS.**

➤ 2. **MAKE A LIST OF THE EQUIPMENT YOU NEED.**

➤ 3. **CARRY A REMINDER WITH YOU TO KEEP YOU ON COURSE.**

CHAPTER FIVE

TAKE TIME TO DREAM

Daydreaming or night dreaming, pondering or purposeful thinking — all have the authority of God-likeness. The reason I make such a claim is because in any of these exercises something is being developed that was not there before in conscious thinking. Therefore, when you engage in these activities, you join hands, as it were, with the Creator, exhibiting some of His power, validating again that you are made in His image. Why?

Because in dreaming you are creating something out of nothing.

In so doing, you position yourself on the periphery of God-likeness. You become a mini-creator. Without any substance or form, you create an image of an idea or event you intend to pursue, and it will take a tangible shape. The marvelous thing about visualizing, brainstorming and dreaming is — you can trigger them at will, if you keep the mechanism in working order.

Let me take that thought a little further. When my children were small, they would talk to me in detail about all kinds of imaginary events and present me with a multitude of creative thoughts while awake, full of life and involved in adventure. In adulthood, we tend to put the brakes on our dream machine, and as we grow older, the brake is further applied until our dreaming stops. But not so with great entrepreneurs. Throughout life, they continue to paint word pictures from their dreams and thereby inspire others.

I cannot resist pausing and asking here, "Do you get the picture?"

Your dream machine can be turned on again by creative imagination, and you can experience the wonder of the mind in a kaleidoscope of images. So take off the brake and expose yourself again to those wonders you saw as a child, but now see them through the strong, experienced eyes of adulthood.

To set your life goals, you will need to imagine your life and the world up to ten, twenty, thirty, forty, even fifty years into the future. In so doing, excite your senses and reawaken your spirit to the greatness within you.

POINTERS

➤ 1. AWAKEN YOUR DREAM MACHINE.

➤ 2. DREAMING IS ON THE PERIPHERY OF GOD-LIKENESS.

➤ 3. LEARN TO SEEK THE FULL PICTURE.

TOO BUSY TO DREAM

Some people's lives are so involved and so complicated they are too busy to dream.

My son, Peter Jr., who is a director of some of our companies, said to me one afternoon, "Dad, I spent two hours alone in the lounge of the Hilton Hotel this morning imagining and dreaming, and I have come up with forty new ideas." I'm glad he's not too busy to dream, because if he were, he would not be successful today.

Many years ago I was faced with an uncomfortable deficit in my business, and I could not figure out how to handle the problem. I spoke to my office manager, Mrs. Hall, and asked her to go home and come up with an idea that would give us the extra income we needed. She said she was too busy and could not think of anything. But I insisted, requesting that she stay home on full pay until she could think of an imaginative way to solve our dilemma!

"I know you have a simple idea," I said to her, "and I am depending on you to deliver it."

It was not long before Mrs. Hall returned with a plan, one that was so simple it only took ten minutes to implement and begin providing the needed funds.

Don't be too busy to dream, rather be busy dreaming.

Make it a regular habit to reduce your heavy work load and go alone to a quiet spot with a pen and paper or a tape recorder and begin to dream, think, imagine, plan, plot and talk to yourself. It could be the most profitable time in your otherwise hectic schedule.

Another reason some people avoid dreaming is because it is a frightening experience. If seed thoughts are formulated into an idea and then further developed into a project, there is an obligation to do something about them — which presents a challenge to the dreamer's personal comfort zone.

Dreaming is a part of life and a catalyst for the adventurous spirit. To keep it alive is to be fully alive oneself; to dampen its fuse is to dim one's own light.

Remember, goal-setters are never too busy to dream.

POINTERS

> ➤ 1. SLOW DOWN AND DREAM.

> ➤ 2. DON'T BE AFRAID TO DREAM.

> ➤ 3. DREAMING AWAKENS LIFE.

SPEND PRIME TIME DREAMING

It is not a pleasant prospect to reach a point in a hazardous journey and find that you have forgotten something in your planning. Similarly, who of us in life's journey wants to reach a lofty peak only to discover an avalanche of doom descending on us because we did not anticipate the inevitable? I know it is not possible to evaluate all the possibilities, but not to spend prime time trying is to invite disaster.

Dreaming or imagining can provide tremendous value in paving the way to success.

Let me illustrate this point by sharing with you a story about a pastor friend of mine who committed his church congregation to erecting a huge new building. After the architect's plans were approved, the pastor and the church secretary took all the relevant papers and plans and laid them out on a large table. Then they decided to do something quite unique. They agreed to imagine that the building was finished. Together they would visualize the completed structure and "walk" through it to see if it suited their needs.

The first thing they did (in their imagination) was to unlock the door and started to switch on the lights. When they compared their imaginative picture with the plans laid before them, they discovered that the architect had placed the light switch thirty feet from the front entrance! Alteration number one prevented them from having to open the church with a flashlight!

Next on their imaginary tour they walked into the foyer where they expected to see a beautiful flower arrangement on the table or paintings on the walls. They checked the plans and found that the fire hydrants were situated in the corridor facing the front door. Alteration number two: Change the position of the fire hydrants.

So the process went on as they made their way throughout the entire structure. By the end of their imaginary visit, alterations had been made improving acoustics, layout and many other aspects of the proposed building. All these things came about because they spent prime time dreaming.

Get into the habit of testing out your projects by using the wonders of active imagination.

POINTERS

➤ 1. **DREAMING DOESN'T WASTE TIME, IT SAVES TIME.**

➤ 2. **DEVELOP THE PRIME-TIME HABIT.**

➤ 3. **TEST YOUR PROJECT BY DREAMING.**

DREAMING IS REALITY

There is absolutely nothing capricious in God's nature. This includes dreaming, because dreaming illustrates hidden capacities and unawakened abilities. There is no reason for God to give us human beings the capacity to imagine and dream positively and creatively without expecting us to realize our dreams and complete our tasks. Just as you and I have the great power of choice to select the dream we follow, so we have the ability to direct our creative imagination to dream the dreams we want to achieve.

But be alert to the elusiveness of your dreams and document their course; otherwise, you will miss the dynamic, fleeting thought you felt so powerfully. You may never expect to lose it, but if you don't secure it, you will.

I have been waiting for years to recapture a thought on a major breakthrough in behavioral science I discovered and documented (only to lose the paper and with it the recollection of those thoughts). Try as I may over many years, I have never been able to recapture its contents, although a couple of times I have felt I was on the edge of its appearing.

On occasion I awaken in the middle of the night with a thought or an idea, and I leap out of bed, like a man possessed, and stay up for hours writing it down. At these times, my wife will never speak or inquire, because she understands the fragility of such a moment. There have been times when I have completely forgotten about my night's events, only to discover later the evidence of my dream on the writing pad.

At one time I was particularly hard pressed for cash and had arranged for a new product to be manufactured for sale. In my dream one night I saw another item fixed onto the unit, making it not only unique, but also more versatile and practical. The sales from that project saved the day. Dreaming becomes reality when that sort of thing happens.

A dream becomes reality when a person sets out the direction of his dream, documents its response into a plan and then activates the plan to achieve the desired end.

Do you realize that your subconscious accepts your dreams as reality and, in fact, cannot distinguish the difference between a real and an imaginary act?

Let's assume you are asleep and are having a dream in which you are in great danger. Suddenly your mouth becomes dry, your stomach tightens, your legs begin to shake and you start to perspire. Yet nothing has actually happened — or has it? Your subconscious mind and your body react as if the situation were real. In fact, if it were real, your condition would not be much different. Why? Because to the subconscious mind, dreaming is reality.

Daydreaming and imagining, both of which can be either harmful to us or good for us, may eventually draw us like a magnet toward the subject of our thoughts. The Bible says, "As he (a man) thinketh in his heart, so is he" (Prov. 23:7). In that context, we begin to get the picture: We are, or can be, in reality, that which our thoughts make us.

POINTERS

➤ 1. BE CAREFUL, SOME DREAMS DO COME TRUE.

➤ 2. MAKE THE DREAM REAL BY DOCUMENTING IT.

➤ 3. GUIDE YOUR DREAM TIME.

DREAM BELIEVING

If you take your dream time seriously, your dream time will respond seriously. There is no use trying to bridge your integrity gap with pseudo-rationale.

"Belief" is an active word inviting commitment. To activate your imagination and energize your ideas without giving them the credibility of belief is like starting a project without the confidence of its success. Would you employ an executive who had no faith in your marketing plan?

If you cannot believe your dreams, then you should consider smaller dreams or bigger commitments!

To dream and believe requires a certain amount of faith, and in that area a Christian should be prominent, because he accepts the sovereignty of the God Who made him and gave him the capacity to believe and reap the rewards of his belief. Actually, all people have that capacity. It is not exclusive to Christians or any other group. It is a natural component built into man.

Many have been the times I have heard some individual bewail the fact that he once had an idea or a dream but had not been sure it would work and so had done nothing about it. At this point, let me re-emphasize the dream journey procedure described a few pages back: Clarify the dream and "walk through" the project. The subconscious mind accepts a sleeping dream without question. Believing a *waking* dream takes it out of the world of fantasy and puts arms and legs on it.

Take action on your dreams. The idea is to increase your belief by following through those ideas prompted by small dreams. This in turn will establish your belief system through proven results.

POINTERS

> 1. **BELIEF IS CREDIBILITY.**

> 2. **BELIEVING EXPOSES YOUR DREAMS TO SCRUTINY.**

> 3. **BELIEVE SMALL, COMMIT SMALL; BELIEVE BIG, COMMIT BIG.**

DREAM BIG AND FOR A PURPOSE

The reason I recommend big dreams is because I recognize the immeasurable ability in all people. It is something of a revelation to note that no one has ever put accurate limits on a human being, either intellectually or physically. All records are established to be broken; all ideas can be bettered. In discussions I have had with great achievers, I have been told time and again that each one could have gone farther and done better. They all maintain that they could have stretched and expanded because they sincerely believe that boundaries do not exist.

Write this down, it is one of life's truisms: *The distance a person can travel intellectually is directly related to the size of his dreams and the belief he has in them!*

Dream big, and grow, to help those around you grow. Dream big to inspire and improve yourself and others. Dream big to prove that initiative and the democratic way of life can change the course of world events.

Big dreams give purpose, and purpose promotes self-esteem and dignity. There is absolutely no point in wasting a good life, full in years and bursting with promise, on little dreams. Don't limit your life and choke your capacities with small dreams. But following your dreams, turning them into reality, requires another talent, and that is *purpose.*

Many people are still playing their dreams ten years down the road. And I hasten to point out this kind of thing happens not because of a lack of motivation or desire. No, it happens because people don't have purpose.

Let me explain how to determine the presence or absence of purpose. (You can try out this test with your friends.)

Imagine that you are told by someone that he wants to be rich and famous or a great achiever in a specific area. You can tell in a short while whether that special magic is there by asking the individual a simple question: *Why?* You will be staggered at the number of intelligent people who stumble over that question. Often you will discover that it has been only vaguely considered, if any thought has been given to it at all.

To want something for its own sake will provide the launching pad for corner-cutting, manipulation and use or misuse of other people for reasons of selfish greed. An unprincipled nature will limit the dream and certainly sour the prize. Purpose in dreaming puts the emphasis on the reason for achieving, and that is a point that should be remembered.

If you and I pursue a dream for self-grandeur or self-edification, we will naturally exclude those we love and should help; we will veto their participation in the great race. The purpose of a dream and its attainment, for a Christian specifically, must include benefit or help for others, which will uplift and demonstrate principles of faith. In dreaming and planning, the honesty factor must be totally clean and the value system reaffirmed at all levels.

During my early years in business, my son Peter brought me business propositions he thought were workable and full of opportunity. He would explain the proposal with comments like, "But if we could get this price, or if we could buy the product a little cheaper (or if this happened or that happened), then we could make a profit."

My response was always the same, "Son, do not try to force a profit into anything, because it will invariably force its way out again."

65

After more than twenty-five years in business, I have found that a profit forced is a profit I do not want. I would like to say with all conviction that a purpose forced into a dream — however worthy that purpose may seem to be — is unworthy of any dream.

Clear out of your mind selfishness, greed, gain for gains' sake and any thought of manipulating others or the system. Instead, dream a dream full of purpose, pure of intent and big in dimensions, one that will honor God and yourself and inspire all who participate in it.

POINTERS

➤ 1. YOUR CAPACITY IS IMMEASURABLE.

➤ 2. DON'T WASTE TIME ON LITTLE DREAMS.

➤ 3. REMEMBER THAT DREAMING EXPANDS CAPACITY.

➤ 4. CLARIFY YOUR PURPOSE.

➤ 5. NEVER FORCE A PURPOSE INTO A DREAM.

➤ 6. MAKE YOUR PURPOSE BIG ENOUGH TO INCLUDE OTHERS.

DREAM ON PAPER — NAIL DOWN THE DREAM

To pull a dream down from the shelves of the mind onto the workbench of reality requires a nail down of ideas and thoughts on the clean framework of the written page. And this is where the foggy, the frail and the flamboyant collapse in a heap.

A dream unfulfilled is just a childish fancy.

If you are the least bit serious about your dream, solidarity of documentation and clarity of examination must be worked into it. Write it in a relaxed, conversational way without judgment, embellishment or qualification.

Go into detail and include any new thoughts or ideas as you write. Decide that you will not show this documentation to any other soul. At the same time fight back any thoughts of how others may react, what they may say or feel about that dream which is now taking shape. As you work, allow maximum time for writing and minimum time for reason, thought or reflection as you begin to cross the boundary from fantasy to reality. Do not read or correct the dream of your life goals until you have exhausted all your thoughts and recorded everything you want to write.

If you find you lose the flow, for whatever reason, stop and come back to it in a few days — although there is a risk that by then you may have "reasoned out" some of the great thoughts. The second time around you may have to wait for that special mood or feeling before you can try again.

POINTERS

➤ 1. **GET THE VAPOR ON THE PAPER.**

➤ 2. **DON'T REASON THE DREAM.**

➤ 3. **DON'T INTERRUPT THE DREAM.**

REMOVE THE NIGHTMARES

At some time or other we all have had to face nightmares, those unspoken fears that bubble up from the deep recesses of the mind and jolt us into a waking sweat.

Psychologists and psychiatrists have probed nightmares and come up with a variety of explanations for them ranging from childhood terror to something eaten just before bedtime!

So how can you remove the nightmare from your dreams and reach your life goals? First, remember that it is the areas of doubt within the dream that create the nightmare, the fear, the uncertainty.

67

Examine now the dream you have committed to paper and add reality and reason in the areas of doubt. Bear in mind that you have to come to grips with the areas in your dream that present uncertainty.

For example, if you are going to be involved in important money matters, but know nothing about this field, you must learn the basics of high finance. If the fulfillment of your dream requires high levels of persuasion, then you must learn to sell, or develop the ability to select and elicit loyalty from others who will work with you.

The thing to watch for is cheap advice or experience that in the long run becomes expensive. Even expensive advice may not provide the expected return for the outlay. Do not cut corners and do not accept bad advice. Easy to say, maybe. So let us now simplify the selection process.

Let's take, for example, the field of real estate, with which I am familiar. If you are going to invest in a piece of property, to whom should you go for advice? The property owner? Naturally not, he has a vested interest. The bank manager? No, because he has disqualified himself by placing himself under bank supervision; besides, if he understood the investment you are considering, he would be involved in it himself. An accountant? No, accountants keep the score; they don't make the goals. An investment adviser? This could be the person, but you will do well to check him out carefully. A successful businessman? Yes, but put your cash on the table and pay for his advice if necessary. It may be the best you will ever get.

In the long run, the best person to seek advice from is yourself. Through careful thought, and after sifting and sorting through all the data, weigh the pluses and minuses.

The final decision is yours, and the results — good or bad — are yours to enjoy, or endure.

But make a decision by choice and not by circumstance. Don't wait until all of your questions have been answered, because there will be some that will never be answered. To procrastinate is to stagnate. Remember that guarantees are not available in dreams.

A hunch, or a "gut feeling," rarely overrides or changes facts, but its presence is not to be ignored because it can be a confirmation that you are on the right track. If you make a decision, you are immediately on the move toward your life goals. If you have cleared the debris by clarifying areas of doubt and confirming areas of action, then you are well on you way to polishing your dream.

POINTERS

➤ 1. **TEST YOUR DREAM FOR PROBLEM AREAS.**

➤ 2. **RECOGNIZE THAT NIGHTMARES ARE UNRESOLVED PROBLEMS AND NEED TO BE REMOVED.**

➤ 3. **CHECK THE SOURCE OF ADVICE AS WELL AS THE ADVICE ITSELF.**

➤ 4. **REMEMBER, A GOOD HUNCH OR "GUT-FEELING" MUST BE TAKEN INTO CONSIDERATION.**

THREE DAYS OF PAPER DREAMS

Many years ago, when I was desperate to understand the principles of goal-setting but couldn't find anyone or any book to help me, I devised a plan to get my life together. I would recommend it only to the very desperate, those who cannot cope any other way. It is exhausting, time-consuming and more than a little different. But, nevertheless, it was what I needed at the time, and it solidified my life for the next ten years.

Go to a place where there are no telephones, television sets, newspapers, radios or people. Take with you sufficient food and other requirements for at least three days. Add to that provision a quantity of large plain white sheets of paper and drawing pens.

On day number one accept in your imagination that you and the world are ten years older. Draw, at random, homes, automobiles, fashions and anything else that comes to your mind, picturing them as they may be ten years from now. Include matters of politics, world events, science, travel, economics and anything else that comes into your mind. Think intently about your own physical, mental and spiritual well-being on the basis that you are ten years older. Do not stray from that path of thought and concentrate! Concentrate! Concentrate!

By the time you go to bed tired that night, you should have some impression in your conscious and unconscious thinking that the immediate worries you had are passed, your early limitations have been breached, the world and you have both moved ahead — and you are successful. This mental experience needs to be your last thought before you go to sleep ready for the morning and phase two.

The next day, having accepted that you are ten years older, turn your thoughts to your imaginary achievements over the past ten years. Write down where you went and what you did and how you overcame all difficulties. Detail how you developed your plans and met your goals. Describe the pinnacles you reached and the rewards that were yours. How did those around you benefit? Write down in some detail how you feel with that kind of accomplishment under your belt, and do it with conviction and embellishment. Let your mind soar as you write. Then have a restful night enjoying the exhilaration of the dream achievement.

On day three, you are back to reality and square one, or are you? My guess is that you have experienced the same thing I experienced during my three-day dream session. If so, you will never be quite the same again. Your boundaries have been enlarged, and you are ready for the challenge of reality. Now set your next ten years' goals on the basis of your previous two days' experience with the optimism of having role-played the scene and been through the entire procedure before. Do not minimize the importance or significance of such an experience nor play down the enormity of the task ahead, but use its dynamics to thrust you toward the attainment of your dream.

In my own life, I used these principles, and I exceeded my goals in my ten-year plan beyond what I imagined, let alone what I had written down. I believe that your response will be in direct proportion to the serious way you apply yourself to its truths.

POINTERS

➤ 1. IMAGINE THAT YOU ARE TEN YEARS OLDER.

➤ 2. IMAGINE WHAT YOU HAVE ACHIEVED IN THOSE TEN YEARS.

➤ 3. WRITE DOWN YOUR TEN-YEAR GOALS ON THE BASIS OF THAT EXPERIENCE.

PUT LIFE INTO YOUR DREAMS

To put life into your dreams, you must first break out of the dream cocoon. The dream cocoon has all of the comforts of the dream, but none of its obligations. It is in the cocoon, devoid of exercise and air, that most dreams stay and die. Your dream must be more than a vision confined in a cage of thought. It must, if it is to be realized, force the door of the cage and demand the challenge only found in the real world. If it dies in its delivery, or on the workbench, then it either has to be put back to incubate or allowed to crumble.

Some dreams do need more incubation than others, and other dreams need more sustenance and care in the infancy stages because they are sick with problems. You have read in the previous chapters that a dream must have the permanence of paper, and with that permanence comes the opportunity to give it life and exposure to justify its existence.

Now is the time to make your dream part of your every moment by affirming continually and relentlessly its existence, its purpose and its destination. As you become involved with the mundane habits of life that beset us all, the dream must be lived in that context and in all of those moments. Your thoughts each new day must involve regular thinking about your dream. The life that you put into your dream by affirmation and enthusiasm will eventually capture you in its net. It will be noticed by others who are close to you. Very soon you will discover that they are talking about it with you and with others because of the attraction and inspiration you give the dream by the very breath you breathe into it.

Your dream or goal can only exist while you give it life.

Your daily, weekly, monthly and yearly association with your dream will produce enormous returns if you keep feeding it with your enthusiasm, action and love. But it must have your commitment and closeness to develop its triumphant spirit, and at times you may have to coax it forward to victory. Be prepared to nurse it when it seems frail, to activate it when it seems lazy and to boost it even further when it is in progress. Never leave it alone for any length of time without paying attention to its requirements. Without you, it is feeble and frail and can, if neglected, slip into oblivion only to be taken up by someone else who is prepared to carry it through.

Somewhere down the road you may come across a piece of paper written many years earlier about a dream that could have been a magnificent obsession, lost through the sluice gates of apathy, neglect or indifference. Yet your dream belongs only to you and is only achievable while you give it life. In giving it life, you ensure its destiny.

POINTERS

➤ 1. **BREAK OUT OF THE DREAM COCOON.**

➤ 2. ACCEPT THAT ONLY YOU CAN GIVE YOUR DREAM LIFE.

➤ 3. LIVE THE DREAM TO ITS ULTIMATE DESTINY.

PLAN AND WORK THE DREAM

The planning of your goals should be exciting because you are dealing with your own destiny, exercising the awesome power of choice and documenting the timing and process of action. Planning is a means. The means may change from time to time, but you will never change the ultimate goals of your life plan. Nevertheless, planning is important.

This process of planning must include an assessment and evaluation of all aspects of your strategy and a documentation in detail of the path you need to follow. The direction that will be taken, together with the provisions of knowledge, people, location and timing, all relate to the ultimate destination.

At first, *particular attention should be paid to time*. Every goal has a time frame to which everything else must conform. To have a goal without clarity of timing is to move back into the zone of wishful thinking and away from objective and determined planning. Spend prime time evaluating carefully and determining precisely the ultimate date for reaching your goal, carefully considering all aspects including your age, the projected economic and political climate and social trends.

Next, *deal with supportive goals*, such as the meeting of capital and mental and logistical requirements in relation to a time frame. Take into consideration the start-up factors involved in achieving your life goals.

Suddenly your goals take form. You have the supportive building blocks to reach the summit. Do a countdown in all areas including minor goals and the supportive requirements needed to reach them. Draw up timetables and achievement levels which must be reached before further progress can be made.

This planning of your goals, step by step, time partition by time partition, will provide a working chart that will ultimately allow you to re-evaluate and reorganize your original plan, because it now has time and form which can be objectively analyzed.

POINTERS

➤ 1. **PLANNING GIVES FORM TO YOUR DREAMS.**

➤ 2. **TIMETABLES AND TIME FRAMES PROVIDE THE STRUCTURE FOR COMPLETION.**

➤ 3. **DO A COUNTDOWN IN ALL AREAS TO COMPLETE YOUR PLANS.**

The plan is now in its elementary form and must be put to the test in the real world. At this point the shine and the glow lose some of their luster as hard reality sets in. Whatever you do, don't change the plan just because you experience some hard knocks, disappointments or setbacks, because it is at this point that the dream is confirmed.

No dream in reality goes as easily as the visionary dream. That is why so much time was spent in previous chapters, clarifying, sorting and confirming. It is at this point that you realize just how much of a nightmare and illusion you have removed from your dream.

Working a dream becomes a real test of endurance, patience and faith.

It weeds out the casual and the theoretical philosopher from the pragmatic worker who is expecting, willing and eager to pay the price and endure the pain. At this time again your value system will be tested and your pain endurance proved for the climb to the summit.

Working a dream means putting in whatever time and effort is necessary to make it succeed.

There is a big difference between activity and productivity. Many salesmen today think that all they have to do to succeed is to present their goods to prospective customers. Not so. To be a success in sales, a person must call on as many potential customers as possible and tell them all the right things about the product or service being offered.

Hard work alone will not win the day. Working your dream until you drop may not achieve anything unless you prepare yourself in whatever way necessary to complete the job. The first essential is to work on yourself relentlessly.

I once knew a man who had a huge goal. He spent thirty days with every book he could find on the subject. He spent hours on the phone chasing down every single item on which he needed more information. He worked his plan by realizing that he himself was the most important component of it. The thirty days he spent alone in the early stages pushed him light years ahead of others who were attempting to do the same thing he was doing.

So, with the early skills in order, attack your minor goals and deadlines with enthusiasm, knowing that the action starts and ends with you! Like a moon rocket which uses most of its fuel at lift-off, and then requires less energy after it passes the earth's gravitational pull, you will find that getting launched is the hardest part.

In my case, I did not prepare myself completely in the early years, so I had to suffer the discomfort of going broke three times before I learned the lessons I needed for success. In so doing, I was able to develop a more reliable tool — myself — to get the job done.

You may have some false starts and setbacks, but to the sincere goal-achiever and dream-maker these are only temporary. After many years on the road, such hindrances fade into minor irritations that have to be endured in order to experience success.

Never allow yourself to make excuses, like thinking you are "too honest to succeed." In working your plan you will find yourself looking for alibis or scape goats when things start to go wrong. If you look anywhere else but to yourself and your plans, you are doomed to failure.

POINTERS

➤ 1. **YOU ARE THE FIRST THING TO WORK ON.**

➤ 2. **DON'T CONFUSE FALSE STARTS AND DELAYS WITH FAILURE.**

➤ 3. **NEVER LOOK FOR EXCUSES TO EXPLAIN THE FAILURE — INSTEAD SEEK TO FIND AND SOLVE THE PROBLEM.**

EXPAND THE DREAM

One of the continued surprises of my life is that goals and dreams continue to expand. As one avenue of endeavor opens up, another opens as well. The more that is done, the more there will be to do — and it will usually be more exciting and interesting than the tasks that went before it.

As you start to work your dream by first working on yourself, you will discover that you have other abilities. The process, it seems, goes on throughout life. Opportunities continue coming forward offering further incentive and challenge to meet life goals.

The chances of attaining your life dreams are good; the chances of exceeding them are overwhelming.

You will be compelled time and time again to ask yourself these two questions: 1) Why didn't I think of it before? and, 2) Can I expect much more? The answer to the latter is yes, because you are no longer indecisive, hesitant and without clear purpose. You are now on a firm course and moving toward a predetermined destination, one which you yourself have chosen.

Under this kind of posture you cannot help but discover changes in your personality and character as you develop attitudes and interests in different areas. Any expansion of your dream must take as its pivot point your ultimate goal. You must not veer from your course, however fanciful the temptation may seem at the time.

I have seen many goals and dreams shattered by distraction or diversion of interest under all kinds of good and even benevolent disguises. Too often, the unsuspecting goal-setter ends up totally off course and a long way from his goal before he ever realizes the bitterness of distraction.

You move away from your ultimate goal at your own peril. However, some changes may be made after careful examination to enhance and speed up the process. Make sure any changes are tested and proven, usefully and successfully, before commitment. Expand your goal carefully and avoid doing so while you are under stress or on the crest of a wave. During such times your emotions can be on full throttle, and emotion in any person has a bad history in relation to integrity.

POINTERS

➤ 1. **AS YOU GROW, YOUR DREAM WILL GROW.**

➤ 2. **ALLOW YOUR DREAM TO EXPAND.**

➤ 3. **DON'T CHANGE DIRECTION WITHOUT INSPECTION.**

In fact, early disappointment can be very helpful by calling attention to an unrecognized problem, thus preventing a huge catastrophe farther down the road. So treat disappointment as a friend, acknowledging its reality, examining its credentials and considering its impact as an act of preventive medicine for the future.

Resurrect whatever you can from disappointment as there are always bits and pieces that can be put back into the mainstream of your dream. If you look at it carefully with a positive attitude, and if you use creative imagination, you may even find a way to turn the problem into a propeller. Make use of the painful experiences of life to help you reach your next level of achievement.

POINTERS

➤ 1. **DISAPPOINTMENTS ARE INEVITABLE.**

➤ 2. **YOUR DREAM IS STRONGER THAN YOUR DISAPPOINTMENT.**

➤ 3. **EARLY DISAPPOINTMENTS CAN HELP YOU GET BACK ON COURSE AND REACH YOUR GOALS.**

LEAN ON YOUR DREAM

During times of frustration the only thing left to do may be to "lean on your dream." You know it can hold the weight, and so the best thing to do is simply to hold on to it and wait.

When the going gets tough, lean on your dream and use your ingenuity to create new ideas and opportunities. Stoppages or blockages at any time create frustration, particularly when you know that your plan is sound and that you are doing everything you can to reach your goal. At these times you must concentrate on your dream and focus your attention on your ultimate objective, asking yourself the question, What can I do during this frustrating delay that will act as a catalyst either to remove the object of the frustration or to make use of the frustration and derive a benefit from it?

CHAPTER SIX

DISAPPOINTMENTS, FRUSTRATION AND FAILURE

FRUSTRATION AND CREATIVITY

I remember being delayed one time at an international airport, fogged in with nowhere to go. I sat down and started to think about my life and my behavior. As I did so, I asked myself a series of questions, inquiring, as it were, why I did or did not do certain things. It was a worthy time of self-analysis, and some of the answers I have been able to pass on to many others with some benefit.

I recall on another occasion the way I worked my way out of a seemingly frustrating disappointment with humor and resolve. It was when my car's automatic transmission broke down, and I simply could not afford the repair bill. I was thousands of miles from my destination and had to get there to keep my business going.

The mechanic laid out all the pieces on the cement floor and said, "The whole transmission is worn out and needs completely replacing." When he quoted the figure I went into orbit. I could not pay it, and I was in deep despair.

Then I did a remarkable thing. I leaned on my dream and resolved to get that car fixed and hit the road. I reasoned that it would be impossible for every part of my transmission to be totally worn out. I knew zero about cars. So I figured I would speak to the mechanic in ignorance — with a dash of humor — and check out the answer to some questions.

I examined each part of the transmission with the mechanic following me. I asked him could he weld this? Expand that? File this? Replace that and pack it with washers? Tighten this? Put springs on that? Get a secondhand piece to put in? I reached the point where the mechanic was in fits of laughter, and in a good-humored way, he joined in the fun with suggestions and alterations.

The end result was that I got back into my car for a fraction of the cost and reached my scheduled destination. (Incidentally, I sold that car with another sixty thousand miles on the clock, and the transmission was as strong as ever!)

Believe that frustration and seeming failure can be a time of creativity and learning.

DISAPPOINTMENT AS CHALLENGE

Disappointments are the testing times. They provide opportunities to evaluate resolves and test the determination quotient before the next step. During times of disappointment, attitude is of paramount importance, because it is at that level that enthusiasm can be accelerated or deflated.

The handling of your first disappointment should be accepted as a direct challenge to your ultimate goal and your personal management ability. Evaluate its occurrence and results just as you would if you were a probing scientist.

POINTERS

➤ 1. FRUSTRATION CAN BE TIME-CREATING.

➤ 2. FRUSTRATION CAN BE A TIME OF REASSESSMENT.

➤ 3. **FRUSTRATION CAN FORCE THE DEVELOPMENT OF PERSISTENCE AND PERCEPTIVE POWERS.**

FAILURE IS TEMPORARY

Failure all too often brings with it the incriminating accusation of worthlessness. It can be fiendishly judgmental or devastatingly humiliating, and it often sows the seeds of doubt.

It is true that success tends to smooth the memory of doubt and failure. Conversely, failure brings the feeling of worthlessness.

At one time when I failed I had nothing but a mountain of debts — equivalent to five years' salary for a top executive. I also had no job and no opportunity with which to attack the problems. But I had a dream that was still real and vivid in my mind, and though I was utterly exhausted, I used that dream to get on my feet, grease the wheels and affirm life goals with God's call and hand upon my life.

During those difficult months with creditors, I was smiling deep down inside because I could still see the fulfilled dream, the complete picture. I handled that catastrophe by putting it into its limited time frame and by leaning on my dream.

Any failure is only a temporary setback that will appear from the most unlikely of places and through the most unlikely of circumstances, but the stronger you cling to that dream the easier it is to push through.

Remember, you are only a permanent failure when you have decided to give up.

POINTERS

➤ 1. **DREAMS CAN ACT AS PROTECTIVE BARRIERS AGAINST FAILURE.**

➤ 2. **FAILURE IS ONLY A TEMPORARY CONDITION.**

➤ 3. **FAILURE CAN BE A STEP UP.**

REASSESSMENT

There will come a time of reassessment and reflection when you will ask yourself the question: *Is it all worth it*, and am I on the right track? The important point to remember here is that you are still talking about means, not about your final destination. Rarely will the life goal come into question. The real question is: *Will I reach my goal*, and am I on the right track?

Times of reassessment can be good because they force you again to evaluate your progress and to reconsider the methods you are applying to reach your goal.

Now is the time to reaffirm your ultimate dream and relive it.

The focus must always be on the life goal.

In your assessment, be factual about your accomplishments so far. If they are minimal, examine the reasons why in detail. Pay particular attention to your own performance. (You may like to read my book *How To Be Happy Though Rich* to get some more help). Small achievements cannot be measured on the basis of their immediate returns but rather on the basis of the lessons learned and the effect they have had, and will have, upon you personally.

Examine your time frames and see if they need some readjustment. Look for obsolete items that are no longer applicable to your overall goal. Seek to streamline the process and look for legitimate shortcuts that will allow you to catch up on your timetable without impairing the whole program.

Also search for innovations or recently discovered methods that could render your existing path obsolete, or new machinery that could save time or provide more information. Find out if you can develop a new method of financing to enable you to take a quantum leap without putting yourself at risk. New and faster methods can be adopted to do all kinds of things over the coming years, and when they appear, you may say, "Why didn't I think of that?"

Use your fantastic ability to think and test new ideas by role-playing them in your mind. If successful, you will find you have used your time of reassessment to thrust forward rather than to sink into a rut. Use this important period of your life to uphold your dream and iron out problem areas. Areas of doubt should be dealt with and attacked with positive vigor. Don't put off or ignore the reassessment, but rather greet the opportunity with positive expectancy.

It takes a certain amount of courage to face a reassessment, so in that respect it should be welcomed as a true friend.

POINTERS

➤ 1. **REASSESSMENT CAN BE VERY HELPFUL.**

➤ 2. **REASSESSMENT CAN STRENGTHEN YOUR RESOLVE.**

➤ 3. **REASSESSMENT IS REAFFIRMING.**

CHAPTER SEVEN

WHY GOALS FOR LIFE?

LIFE AND TIME

Everyone has been given the gift called life, although some keep it longer than others. Many measure life by its duration and hope and pray for longevity with health to enjoy its benefits. Some may look back on their life's journey with regret and disappointment, while others see it as a bland series of events moving toward an uneventful end.

Life must be measured in something more meaningful than time.

Surely life is more than that.

Some people come and go in a short lifetime, but manage to leave an indelible mark on history which affects the lives of generations to come. Jesus Christ changed the course of history, and yet His earthly time with us was limited to thirty-three years. The time frame you and I have been given here on earth has not been revealed to us. But putting aside accidental death, life is continually being extended by medical science, and seventy years is now the average limit.

But even our doctors can be wrong in assessing termination of life under what they consider clear and predictable circumstances.

Many years ago my wife and I were called to the doctor's office and were told that my wife's mother could not hope to live out the year because her heart was in such bad condition. She lived on another ten years and contributed greatly to others around her. I believe the extension was in relationship to her dreams.

You have been given your life, whatever its time frame, to use wisely and well. Not in subjective form but in objective form to achieve and to grow for your benefit and the benefit of others. To trade that opportunity for a limited goal over a limited time frame, and not to use it for its full measure, is in effect to reject its usefulness and its worth.

Over the years I have noticed that those who retire and have no further goals die or are confined to total medical care within a few short years. But those who retire in a positive way seem to slip into another gear and another role and get a new lease of life and activity in the process. They extend their lives even farther.

The real high-flyers are those who have the magnificent obsession that could be expanded to a thousand years. They strive, plan, stretch until their last breath, enjoying life to the hilt.

A short life shut down in the middle of a goal still leaves behind a level of commitment reached, and something else — an inspiration for those who were fortunate enough to have known and worked with the person concerned.

Having said all of that, let me add that life's time frame is still relatively predictable and the number reaching senior years is growing considerably every decade. So you are on the side of predictability, and your chances of surviving to old age are almost guaranteed.

POINTERS

➤ 1. **LIFE'S TIME FRAME IS WEIGHTED HEAVILY ON THE SIDE OF LONGEVITY.**

➤ 2. LIFE GOALS GIVE AND EXTEND LIFE.

➤ 3. LIFE MUST BE MEASURED IN DOING, NOT DYING.

SECOND BEST?

Short little spurts of energy and hesitant steps to progress along with short-term, limited goals are really second best. A goal for, say, two years, or even ten years, without a master plan for life, leaves no room for hope and no hope for room. To accept short-term assignments throughout life is to take life in little nibbles, never savoring the banquet.

To have your life limited by accident or illness is one thing. To limit your own life is something quite different. Accident or illness may take the situation out of your hands, but self-limitation squashes its potential. You never realize the enormity of the opportunities before you. Cutting your life up into little pieces without a grand plan is stifling your achievement quotient. It may give variety, but it rarely gives satisfaction.

With a life goal comes variety. You could, of course, have a life goal made up of many small goals, which would give you a series of goals and achievement timetables, but for what purpose? You see, purpose for living must be included; when it is, you are back on the track of setting life goals. Then you are walking in unison with what you were created for.

Accepting second best is an admittance of perpetual failure, but the tide is so easily turned by just focusing attention on the ultimate goal or purpose.

Maybe you consider it selfish to program your life to achieve a magnificent obsession. So why not take the focus off yourself and put it on your achievement for someone or something else?

Taking life seriously glorifies God; taking life flippantly glorifies man.

Setting goals for life with purpose and commitment guarantees benefits and progress to all. Protecting oneself from long-term commitment and purpose is wasting life and abandoning responsibility to all mankind.

All of us must, if we are to exhibit integrity, pull our fair share of the load. By opting out of goals for life, we waste our abilities and opportunities, and therefore accept second best.

Our best cannot be done by someone else! It is unique to us individually and only "cashable" by us personally; not to spend it means that the world is the poorer. We should not measure ourselves against others by direct comparisons because we are all different. But we can consider others who have not been blessed with some of our gifts and opportunities and yet who have surpassed us in their achievements. We can evaluate ourselves *with* — not *against* — others.

Second best shrivels up character. When we accept it as our goal, we are saying to our children, "Here is the benchmark I have set as a standard for you. Don't go beyond it — second best is good enough for us."

Our family and friends will recognize the benchmark we have set in our life, and if it is not high enough we will recognize our failure and folly.

Second best is not good enough — life is worth our best effort, and we need to be committed to plan for it.

POINTERS

➤ 1. SECOND BEST IS A SELF-PUTDOWN.

➤ 2. SECOND BEST IS A POOR BENCHMARK FOR OTHERS.

➤ 3. SECOND BEST IS NOT DIRECTLY A MEASUREMENT.

COMMITMENT LEVEL

I was driving in my car with a long-time friend, but my mind was away thinking and "strategizing."

"Peter, you're not really here," my friend said. "What in the world are you thinking about?"

I told him that I was trying to work out how I could get more done, fit more into my life plan and achieve more than I had been achieving.

"How in the world do you expect to get anything more done?" he responded. "You already have out-stripped and out-performed everyone I know. You are already achieving more in a day than I am achieving in a week. When you talk like that you just make me feel tired."

My friend made the same mistake that many of us make, and that is accepting that a commitment level is full when it really isn't.

The fact is, a commitment level is expandable and its size cannot be measured.

Commitment has no relationship to time, and therefore cannot be harnessed in a time frame. The mistake most people make on the commitment level is this: They put restraints on it that are unrelated to it and try to make it work within boundaries and laws which apply to something else.

Your time commitment may be full — but I doubt it. You can always rearrange and improve it. But your commitment level has to do with something much less tangible, because commitment concerns integrity, life's personal principles and value systems.

Commitment level is often measured by "busyness" rather than progress. Being committed to a project, person or organization must have the measure of objectivity placed against it. Against that criterion, dare I suggest that your commitment level is not really full?

The next question is: Does it have to be full? Which brings up another pertinent question: Exactly what is "full"?

I don't regard your commitment level to be full if it is overflowing to the point of frustration and panic; and I certainly don't consider it full if you're coasting along. I do say it is full when you honestly believe that you are using your commitment level wisely and are doing all you can where you are within the perimeters of your life goals and personal integrity.

To waste a portion of your commitment level is to waste life, and to waste life is wrong indeed. If you are doing things with absolute integrity, you will find that your commitment level will automatically expand itself when a great opportunity or need occurs.

Commitments keep us growing and stretching, and when we grow and stretch in a new direction, we enter the most rewarding and interesting areas of life.

Some years ago a young couple came to me for help in the area of planning meetings — they wanted to be first-rate convention organizers. We discussed the commitment required, and they responded, yes, they thought their commitment level was already full. But they saw a need and wanted to meet that need. Together we arranged for bigger meetings than they had ever organized and in stretching to meet that commitment, they never once went back to their previous level. Their commitment boundaries were expanded. Almost every time I meet them now, I see their boundaries extended even farther.

POINTERS

➤ 1. COMMITMENT BOUNDARIES CAN BE WIDENED.

➤ 2. COMMITMENT MUST NOT BE CONFUSED WITH TIME.

➤ 3. COMMITMENTS ONCE MADE GUARANTEE GROWTH.

WHAT WOULD YOU BE PREPARED TO TRADE YOUR LIFE FOR?

Is an unplanned life better than a planned life? Ask yourself that question and then check what principles you base your answer on. Would you jump on a jumbo jet and zoom off around the world without planning where you were going? Would you let a brain surgeon operate on you, knowing he was just going to "feel his way through" and make up his mind as he went? Of course not! That's preposterous.

But wait, it's not really, because in each case we are dealing with life, and in many instances we are prone to wander along without purpose. Without life goals, there is no purpose.

If all you are going to do is drift along like a rudderless ship, why not trade that life in and get another — one that has purpose and dignity and will benefit others? I see that trade as a bargain, and the price is commitment. What you receive in the trade is a coming alive to the possibilities of your own growth, and in so doing you help others to grow. Most important, you are creating self-worth because you are reaching out from yourself to lift the needy and disadvantaged of the world. Is that not better than self-indulgence or trading off for a lower value?

Your life is valuable, and the use to which you put it increases its value.

With inherent gifts and developed skills, life brings with it a grateful spirit directed by a loving God Who cares for you and is committed to your development. He is blessed by your accomplishment.

POINTERS

> 1. LIFE CANNOT ACCEPT ANYTHING LESS THAN ITS EQUIV-ALENT.

> 2. WITHOUT LIFE GOALS, YOU CHEAPEN LIFE'S VALUE.

> 3. WITH LIFE GOALS, YOU REALIZE LIFE'S WORTH.

EXAMPLES OF LIFE GOALS

The Bible has sharply defined principles for us to follow, and secular investigation and scientific research have never weakened its authority. On the contrary, they have reinforced biblical history with each new discovery. And it is interesting to note that God gave His chosen servants goals for life.

Abraham was given a life goal, and it was promised, under obedience, that it would continue for generations to come.

Moses was given a life goal to deliver the Israelites to the Promised Land; only at the point of that delivery were his life and task finished.

Saul was made king and, although he disobeyed God, was never harmed or even threatened by David, his divinely chosen successor. Saul's anointing could not be removed because of the sacredness of his life goal.

David was given a life goal which he fulfilled.

Hannah had a life goal for her son, Samuel, and with God's help he marched through the pages of biblical history as a prophet, demonstrating his life's call.

Joseph was given a life goal and through ridicule, suffering and opposition, he reached it.

Add to these so many more who were given life goals by God — Samson, John the Baptist, Peter the fisherman, Jonah — and finally, Jesus Christ, Whose goal was our salvation. The abundance of goal-setters in biblical history should be a guide and example to us all, and confirm its commission from the Almighty Father.

POINTERS

➤ 1. GOD GAVE LIFE GOALS IN BIBLICAL TIMES.

➤ 2. **LIFE GOALS CONTROL THE LIFE.**

➤ 3. **LIFE GOALS HAVE A BIBLICAL PATTERN WHICH SHOULD APPLY IN OUR LIVES.**

In addition to the testimony of biblical history, the pages of commercial history are dotted with the famous and the rich who set a life goal, achieving what many thought was impossible.

In Australia we had Sir Sidney Kidman, who as a thirteen-year-old boy with almost no education left home in 1870 for a perilous journey through the barren outback. Only ten years earlier two famous explorers named Burke and Wills had perished in the same area.

Kidman came from a large family and had worked in the cattle yards since he was ten years old. Now, with a one-eyed, aged mare he purchased and called Cyclops, and a half a dollar in savings, he set out to learn the cattle business on the huge livestock farms of Australia. Sidney had a dream which was to focus itself into a life goal to breed and market cattle in the cheap, unpredictable, wild areas of "the land down under." His plan was to establish a string of properties stretching from the north to the south of the continent, following the waterways. This would keep the new colony fed and would expand export markets around the world.

Sidney Kidman became the biggest property owner in the British Empire, and without a doubt the single largest cattle owner in the world at that time. He was affectionately known as "the cattle king." Young Sidney reached his life goals.

W. Clement Stone as a young boy lived without a father, but was blessed with a remarkable mother. From his humble beginnings, by choice and by planned life goals, he became the most respected and the most wealthy life insurance man in the world. I have asked him many times about those early years, and he speaks with confidence and enthusiasm of reaching his life goals. Today he is known as Mr. P.M.A. (Mr. Positive Mental Attitude). Ten minutes in the presence of W. Clement Stone can change a person's life. He deliberately set his life goals and reached them (as this goes to print he is in his nineties and still working).

The late Ray Kroc was a paper cup salesman. At fifty-four years of age he developed a magnificent obsession to buy a hamburger franchise from two brothers called McDonald.

Today it has become one of the largest fast food franchises in the world. Ray Kroc didn't start his life goals until late in life, but within twenty-six years he had reaped a gross annual turnover of one billion dollars. He also is attributed with having made more millionaires than anyone else over the last few decades.

The world of business abounds with stories of real-life situations in which life goals have catapulted ordinary people, with seemingly limited experience and ability, into giants of stature and achievement.

Paul J. Meyer of Success Motivation Institute in Texas is probably the world's leading authority on goal-setting. He has documented stories that make people sit on the edge of their seats with excitement as he unfolds one case history after another of life goal-setters who have achieved and are still achieving the seemingly impossible.

Super business achievers are life goal-setters. They have no limitations on their dreams, and will not tolerate the disturbance or the distraction of little dreams or occasional goals. High achievers plan long and keep short accounts with their own ability: measuring it, coaxing it, upgrading it and progressing it to fit into the context of those life goals.

POINTERS

➤ 1. BIG COMMERCIAL ACHIEVERS SET LIFE GOALS.

➤ 2. LIFE GOALS CAN START AT ANY TIME.

➤ 3. LIFE GOALS ARE DEFINITELY FOR LIFE.

Explorers have a remarkable track record in regard to life-goal commitments, infused as those goals may be with danger, discomfort and disability. From Christopher Columbus to navigator James Cook — who "left nothing unattempted," as it was said — they have come in all sizes, shapes and colors.

Goal-setters today find themselves in space shuttles or probing the deepest oceans. We must occasionally ask ourselves, What is it that pushes them on — fame, fortune or immortality? I don't think it is any of these things, because many of them receive little recognition or remuneration for their efforts.

That strange force that propels man toward life goals crosses cultural and international barriers, confirming that such goals are for the entire human race, both demanded and required.

POINTERS

➤ 1. LIFE GOALS ARE OFTEN ACCEPTED WITHOUT REWARD OR RECOGNITION.

➤ 2. LIFE GOALS FOR MANKIND ARE TRANS-NATIONAL.

➤ 3. LIFE GOALS HAVE BEEN IN EXISTENCE SINCE THE VERY BEGINNING OF RECORDED HISTORY.

SATISFACTION CREATES MOTIVATION

It is a helpless position to be in, wanting to achieve but having nothing worth achieving.

The absence of a goal is probably one of the most destructive forces facing many people today.

To commit your life to something worthwhile will give you the motivation and the energy you need to get the job done.

Motivation does not come from "nowhere" to go "somewhere" — it must come from something specific to go somewhere specific. That drifting feeling comes from a lack of deadlines and an absence of pressure to meet a timetable through a fulfilled commitment.

I hope that reading this book will give you the inspiration towards motivation. But it will never give you motivation.

To become motivated is to invite pressure and commitment.

On a hot, humid summer's day out in the country you do not feel under any compulsion to run or expend any energy, but the sudden appearance of a poisonous snake at your feet propels you into the championship league of the short sprint. You are the same person, in the same place, with the same thoughts, until suddenly you are motivated, compelling you to take action — and action you take!

Life needs pressure. The essence of being motivated is knowing where you are going and knowing that you are on the right track with a compelling desire to get there. The beauty of goal-setting is that its creative force is exclusively personal.

This not only produces satisfaction from knowing where you're going, but it also produces satisfaction by increasing your own self-esteem, and in so doing it creates a self-love that inspires.

In my experience, motivation has only been sustained by an individual who has written life goals with deadlines and measurements, all put together in a parcel that individual believes in.

The most motivated man I have ever met is Dr. John Edmund Haggai, who was so sickly as a child he was not expected to survive. Yet today, in his seventies, he is one of the finest human physical specimens I know.

It has been said by many, "Spend ten minutes on the phone with John Haggai, and you feel you can conquer the world."

John Haggai produces continually, and relentlessly, and persistently, all with good humor. He exudes integrity and has an obvious love for those around him. But John Haggai has a dream, and through the Haggai Institute of Advanced Leadership Training in Singapore, he is rewriting the missionary program and the spiritual history books of Christendom for the whole Third World.

John Haggai has a life goal on paper, with deadlines and a dedicated commitment. How can you stop a man like that? But more important, look at how you can start a man like that.

Life goals are the answer to satisfaction.

POINTERS

➤ 1. SATISFACTION IS KNOWING WHERE YOU ARE GOING.

➤ 2. SATISFACTION CREATES MOTIVATION, AND MOTIVATION INCREASES SATISFACTION.

➤ 3. MOTIVATION MEANS PRESSURE AND COMMITMENT.

PERSONAL GOALS

Have you ever had a great thought, idea or dream about a particular course of action in which you would like to engage? Have you felt the excitement rise as that dream became more clear and the program more realistic? Did you then meditate upon that thought, idea or dream a little more, and realize how great it was and how it could be achieved and so you decided to tell your spouse or friend about it? But as you revealed it with all the excitement of a six-year-old child, were you perhaps faced with a blank stare and a well-mannered, "isn't-that-nice-for-you" response?

Why is it so difficult to transfer a dream to someone else?

The reason is that *a dream is personal.* It is personal because it reflects the sum total of a person's environmental and imaginative experience, and therefore it cannot reflect or produce the experiences of another individual. Goals, too, are deeply personal, but have the added power of emphasis. Goals are the next step to realism. In one giant leap they take an individual from the unreal to the real, still retaining the exclusivity of the dream. And the possibilities of that dream, because of its personal nature, may never be attempted by anyone else; it cannot be duplicated by another.

Do not treat your dreams as if they were community property, but as your very own to protect and cherish and bring to reality.

POINTERS

➤ 1. **DREAMS HAVE THE PRIVACY OF THE INDIVIDUAL.**

➤ 2. **DREAMS, LIKE GOALS, HAVE THE VALIDITY OF BELONGING.**

➤ 3. **DO NOT TREAT YOUR DREAMS LIKE COMMUNITY PROPERTY.**

ENERGY

You know those annoying situations. There you are fatigued and flat, feeling like a wrung-out dishcloth. Then, boom, someone bursts in full of energy and throbbing with action.

The energy quotient of some individuals can leave you gasping, just as the lack of it in others can leave you feeling annoyed. Energy is not as predictable as you may think. A youngster on a school day morning can resemble a snail in reverse gear. But on Saturday morning he is powered on rocket fuel as he dives out of bed, gets dressed in record time and is waiting by the car, football in hand, urging on his half-dressed father.

The remarkable degree of energy available to do what we want to do, would like to do — or by fear are forced to do — gives us some hint of its redeemability.

Energy level does not question the need, but it responds to mental condition and motivation.

There was a time when I considered myself only mildly fit, when some cattle I had bought broke through a fence and strolled into rough country where I had to give chase on foot. I was desperate to get them back, knowing that if they reached a deep gorge I would lose them for keeps. I finally got the stock out, and I returned to the farmhouse exhausted, with my clothes in tatters. When I eventually figured out how far I had run, I estimated I had covered some five miles in heavy clothes over some of the most difficult and steep terrain in the district. If I had been challenged to compete over that sort of country I would have thought it impossible. But, with purpose and strong motivation, I did it.

Energy is personal and can be produced at will in certain circumstances. As you become more experienced at it, you will find you can produce enormous amounts of energy — if the correct circumstances are present.

Your energy thrust, or lack of it, is in direct proportion to your most desired or feared task.

In this context, your life goals can be reached by combining your great dreams with action to ignite that force.

Also remember, your energy level cannot be directly transferred to others, but your enthusiasm and inspiration can help trigger energy in others. Use energy wisely, direct it carefully and acknowledge its usefulness freely.

POINTERS

➤ 1. ENERGY CAN BE EXPANDED, BUT ONLY FOR YOU.

➤ 2. ENERGY COMMITMENT IS YOUR CHOICE.

➤ 3. ENERGY CAN SERVE WELL YOUR LIFE GOALS.

PAIN

Some years ago, I was in hospital in great pain. The doctors were working on me, and I was grunting and groaning with perspiration pouring out of me. I noticed through a gap in the curtain the man in the bed next to me sipping his coffee and reading a book. I wanted to scream out, "Don't you know what I'm going through?" But I knew he couldn't know, and there was no way I could transfer the pain to him!

Yes, well we know it, pain is personal.

When I lost everything and went broke many years ago, I experienced pain which stayed with me in varying degrees for months. My friends could not relate to my suffering. Years later a friend lost everything in a particular deal, and I phoned long distance to speak with him about the pain he was going through.

"You're the first person I've spoken to who understands," he said.

"That's because I once felt it," I replied.

Pain in its isolation indicates our personal responsibility for our own lives and the individual acceptance of our own suffering. The suffering is a deeply personal experience, and the pain endurance (mentioned in a previous chapter of this book) forms a bond between the personal aspects of goal-setting and the personal aspects of pain.

Just as it is impossible to transfer pain, it is also impossible to transfer your life goals to someone else, expecting that individual to feel or endure the pain that comes with his or her own achievements. Certainly pain can be reduced or removed by medication, but in its removal poses the danger of not respecting it — and doing more damage.

Link your life goals to pain. They are personal, felt only by you, not transferable and only avoidable by deadening the relevant area.

Goals demand pain.

Some years ago, during a particularly difficult time in business, I wished I could just go to sleep and wake up twelve months down the road when the difficulties had blown over. Alas, that was not to be, and by experiencing the difficulties — and personally feeling the pain — I became much wiser.

Pain is a warning, a teacher, a protector, and it can be the personal catalyst needed to motivate you to reach your life goals.

POINTERS

➤ 1. PAIN IS ALWAYS PERSONAL.

➤ 2. PAIN CAN ONLY BE UNDERSTOOD BY THOSE WHO HAVE ENDURED IT.

➤ 3. PAIN CAN BE A PERSONAL CATALYST.

LONELINESS

From time to time things will go wrong and, to put it bluntly, you will feel rotten. The depth of your feelings will be directly related to the foolishness or lack of attention to detail that brought about the misery.

From an outsider's point of view you may have seen someone who is suffering and wondered why he or she got so uptight about mistakes in life.

The point is, quite often we blow our mistakes out of proportion, which hurts us more and makes recovery slower. Mistakes, failures and errors of judgment are going to happen from time to time, and we will feel alone. Feeling alone will occur whether we are supported by others or not.

Loneliness is a natural component of life experienced by all who are determined to make something of their lives.

It is not that we disregard the preferred comfort of friends and family. These are always significant assets to us all, and the special bond and affection of a close family is the best support anyone can have. But even with the strongest family or friendship support, the bottom line always exposes itself: It all really depends on us, and we had better get back to the bench quickly, do some repair work and push on.

To wallow in the comfort of friends and family is to slip back farther into failure and despair. Very often what we need is a kick in the pants to increase our fighting spirit, rather than a soft shoulder to cry on.

Don't get me wrong — I know we all need comfort and support from loved ones, but that is to be a temporary thing to dress our wounds and provide us momentary comfort. After a while (and the shorter the time the better), we must get up and go back into battle — bandages, wounds and all — and fight on toward our life goals.

Loneliness in life goals is natural because these goals are ours alone, and we must accept the full responsibility for the results or lack of results. The danger is to think that we can do it all alone, without support and encouragement.

Without family and friends, you must do the next best thing — encourage yourself. And how do you do that? By affirmation, auto-suggestion, reading good inspirational matter (such as biographies) — and of course, prayer.

When the axe does fall, you must take the blow yourself, and assume full responsibility. During such times you may feel what thousands have felt before you: that is, the loneliness of leadership.

For example, if you are in business and something does go wrong, can you tell your bank manager? Of course not! He may well cut off your financial supply. Can you share it with your staff? No, because they are looking to you for solutions, motivation and security. How about sharing it with a competitor? Wrong again. He will be happy to know and take advantage of the setback. Can you tell your spouse? Well, I'm sure that if I told my wife, it would double the trouble because she would start worrying about me.

So let's face it. When things go wrong, loneliness will be a natural component. But for the Christian it creates a strong vertical relationship in prayer with God Himself.

POINTERS

➤ 1. ACCEPT LONELINESS AS A NATURAL COMPONENT OF LIFE.

➤ 2. ACCEPT THE COMFORT OF FAMILY AND FRIENDS AS A BREATHING SPACE ONLY.

➤ 3. NOBODY IS GOING TO FIX THE PROBLEM BUT YOU, SO PUSH ON.

Of course, when things do go right, share the glory and excitement with your family, friends and helpers. In times of victory it is only right that you encourage as much participation as possible. Make the victories in your life goals special occasions because nobody will work faithfully and competently forever without some recognition.

While you are at this point take a back seat, even if you are at the center of attention. Too much involvement in the adoration of the crowd will separate you from your energy and next objective. Relish your victory when you are completely alone, knowing full well that you have set a goal and achieved it.

Victory, like pain and loss, is a personal matter, and no one else can ever quite share in the feelings of the victor.

A point worth mentioning here is that people of high achievement are often accused of being aloof and independent, but I believe that is an unfair generalization. Such an attitude shown by goal-setters and achievers is an expression of their dedication and commitment to a predetermined goal and not necessarily a reflection of their attitude toward other people.

On the victory "high," also guard against making any dramatic shift in your life-goal plan. Wait for a sober moment to reassess if you feel it necessary.

POINTERS

➤ 1. **EVEN IN SUCCESS YOU CAN BE ALONE.**

➤ 2. **SEPARATING YOURSELF FROM OTHERS BECAUSE OF YOUR STRONG COMMITMENT IS AUTOMATIC.**

➤ 3. **DO NOT CHANGE PLANS WHEN YOU ARE ON A VICTORY "HIGH."**

CHAPTER EIGHT

How To Find Goals

YOUR STORY

There are many ways to find life goals. Some people already know theirs, but they have not taken the trouble to verbalize them or put them on to paper for examination.

Throughout this book I have tried to get you acquainted with writing to crystalize your thinking and to give your goals form and substance. The method I am about to suggest is another one I have found helpful, and it may be a valuable tool to clarify your own goals.

In previous chapters I have discussed dreaming, visualizing and imagining as a means of creating and solidifying goals. Now I am going to delve deeper, because I think it will give you some extra clarity.

Think of yourself as being ninety years of age. You have to write your life story.

What will your main theme be?

Is there a particular force in your life that keeps appearing and progressing toward an ultimate, achievable and measurable goal? How will you start your biography after you have gotten through the incidentals of birth, school and other events?

Does a particular thought or objective gnaw at the very root of your life, pestering it and pulling at it, demanding attention for its fulfillment? Can you weave something of a plot through the mystery of your life that has its fulfillment in the recovery of something lost, or the creating of something new or the protection of something good?

Is it possible to get into the story something of perspective and circumstance that makes your heart skip a beat or builds up in you an ache that finally gives way to a sigh of relief upon its discovery?

What will your main theme really be?

Is there anything that you would like to particularly emphasize that would show you in a better light?

How far would you be prepared to embellish that emphasis? What would you be seeking to play down in this biography that you would prefer not to mention or expand upon? How would you describe your habits, morals and relationships with others?

Why not write it down again, not as you see it now, but as you would like it to be? Notice the difference you put on the emphasis and circumstance.

Now you are starting to face up to your life goals.

POINTERS

➤ 1. IMAGINE YOU WERE NINETY YEARS OLD AND WRITING YOUR LIFE STORY.

➤ 2. WHAT WOULD YOUR MAIN THEME BE?

➤ 3. WHAT WOULD YOU PLAY DOWN AND WHAT WOULD YOU EMBELLISH?

➤ 4. USE THIS EXPERIMENT TO CLARIFY YOUR LIFE GOALS.

EMOTION

If you knew for certain that you could achieve your heart's desire, how would you react? Would you be satisfied with keeping it as it is, or would you — knowing of the certainty of its achievement — lose interest in it and choose something extremely different?

Your heart's desire should be examined for emotional stability, with the froth and bubble of sense and feeling removed, to expose the integrity and substance of its existence.

I am not devoid of or against emotion per se, but I am wary of emotion unless I can see the substance of surety or the evidence of fact. Let me illustrate.

I love my family and the evidence is the way I care for them and protect them. The emotional side of my affection is consistent with the evidence of my behavior, and the fact of my consistent support.

With our heart's desire we should express more than just emotional commitment if we want to achieve tangible results.

No one else can commit you to your heart's desire because it has the singular emphasis of your life upon it and, although in some respects others may have similar desires, the attainment of these desires affects each person differently.

Desires are sometimes wishful thinking, usually in the realm of the impossible or the improbable. If we could get our desires, I often wonder how long we would be satisfied. I have known people to have a desire for money, only to find that on attaining it they still do not feel fulfilled. It seems the only form of fulfillment in the realm of money and material possessions is to have just a little bit more.

But if you really want to achieve your heart's desire, why not set it as a goals program with time frames and points for evaluation?

Assess its effect upon you and calculate its purpose in relation to yourself and others. Visualize it, energize it, dream it and give it the permanence of paper.

Some people just don't seem to take these matters seriously. However, the clear evidence is that *if we don't plan anything today, we won't gain anything tomorrow*, because we are today either what circumstances have made of us or what we have made of circumstances.

POINTERS

➤ 1. EXAMINE THE EMOTION IN YOUR DESIRE AND MAKE SURE IT HAS INTEGRITY.

➤ 2. CLARIFY YOUR HEART'S DESIRE AGAINST THE GUARANTEE OF ITS ATTAINMENT.

➤ 3. QUALIFY YOUR HEART'S DESIRE BY SETTING A GOALS PROGRAM.

ETHICS

What if you could fulfil your highest ideals?

Many times in my childhood, and later in my youth, I would hear my friends drift into discussion about their ideals and principles in relation to the adult world, describing what they would do about achieving these ideals if they were adults. Youth is a wonderful time of hope. But it is unfortunate that most of us leave our childhood ideals of fairness, hope and justice back in those years of big dreams when all problems — assuming we were adults — were solvable.

The fact is, many of the problems of life we discussed as youngsters are still solvable, with the application of high ideals and simple logic. But failure, reinforced very often by adults, has worn us down and squashed our potential.

From my childhood and throughout my youth I listened to the dreams of my peers. But, alas, I never saw evidence of achievement.

You may have had the same experience in your own life. If so, why not disturb the slumber of those youthful ideas and weld them with the knowledge you have gained since youth? Take them a few pegs higher and consider their attainment today in the world of business, education and politics. You will find that in reawakening your highest ideals, you are going to open up other areas of thought long since forgotten, and they will become commitments; a new you will begin to emerge forged from your childhood dreams.

POINTERS

➤ 1. YOUR HIGHEST IDEAL IS YOUR BEST YOU.

➤ 2. TAKE PAST YOUTHFUL IDEALS AND WELD THEM TO CURRENT KNOWLEDGE.

➤ 3. OPEN UP NEW THOUGHTS AND IDEAS, AND PEG THEM HIGHER.

PERSONALITY

What if you could choose your own style?

I have described style in a previous chapter in this book. Style is really just a matter of choice. Who among us would not want to choose the style in part or in whole of someone we admire? Oh, to have the dignity and style exhibited by royalty, the confidence and posture of a great statesman, the grace of a professional dancer or the presence of a dramatic actor!

Why not describe your own style in posture, voice and appearance? What would be the highest and best form you could ever devise? Would you like to be able to comfort the distressed like a wise, compassionate pastor or put across your ideas like a highly skilled salesman or entrepreneur? If you knew you could not fail, how far would you go in your requirements and what would you leave out? Why not list the attributes you see as your choice in style, even as far as detailing the kind of deliberate walk you want and the distinctive voice you require?

My friends say they can always tell when I am on television (even when they are not looking), because my voice is distinctive and clear. It did not happen by accident. I was not born with a cultured voice. It was produced by deliberate design and by continual practice every morning for five years with a style in mind, a time frame set for its acquisition and the demands of pitch, pause and projection as my constant companions until it became part of me.

We are really talking about personality because how we project our self is how others will see and respond to us.

Again, in this area of life you have the absolute power of choice. In fact, you can have whatever style you want because it is guaranteed by your choice. Why not consider this aspect of style or personality — visual and audible — as part of your ultimate life goal and give it priority relative to your other goals for life?

We are also setting a pattern of personal clarification that will become our goals.

You already have your own individual style, formed partly by your own personality and partly by picking up habits and postures from others. So why not *choose* your style to complement your other goals and be the best that you can be?

POINTERS

➤ 1. YOUR STYLE IS YOUR CHOICE.

➤ 2. YOUR STYLE CAN BE PROGRAMMED.

➤ 3. YOUR STYLE IS THE YOU THAT YOU WANT TO BE.

GUARANTEED SUCCESS

What would you do if you could guarantee success? The answer to this question will almost explode your mind when you consider its possibilities. To swim the widest river, to climb the highest mountain, to be a billionaire or to achieve fame, recognition or even immortality are possibilities that may flood into your mind.

In the last few pages, we have asked three questions: 1) What if you could achieve your heart's desire? — which refers to emotion; 2) What if you could fulfil your highest ideals? — which refers to ethics; 3) What if you could choose your own style? — which refers to personality. All of these were used to stimulate and provoke attainable goals. But this question of guaranteeing success may seem, at the very least, a little far-fetched. Please stay with me on this track, and let's examine the claim and bring it to reality.

Goals can generally be reached by a careful consideration of four vital factors: 1) the time involved, 2) the ability required, 3) the drive demonstrated by the participant, 4) the opportunity or opposition presented.

The initial factor, the time involved, must have first preference. There is no use in setting a goal to shift a mountain by a certain date, knowing that with all the equipment and manpower available, only a small amount of dirt can be moved in a day's time. The time factor must be of paramount importance and everything must work within its tightly held, unforgiving frame. So our goal, anyone's goal, must respect the confines of time. On that basis we all compete evenly.

The second factor, the ability involved, is somewhat different because ability depends very often on the amount that has to be learned and one's commitment to it. But again we all have to reach our goals on this basis, and any of us can do it if we really want to.

The third factor, the intangible item called drive, can only be measured by demonstration. Given that we have normal physical and mental abilities, the task ahead is our personal responsibility. Again, we are all in the same boat.

The fourth factor, the opportunity or opposition presented, also depends on personal choice. Some people will grab opportunities that others will not. Likewise, opposition will be avoided by some and induced by others. What I am really saying here is that we are all given a fair share. It is like a democracy, where the free enterprise system is encouraged. It is here that we can choose our own goal and plan to reach it with some definite degree of certainty.

So, bearing in mind these four factors of goal-setting, if you could guarantee success, what would you choose as your ultimate life goal?

Remember the earlier advice. Think big and break out of the dream cocoon, then document the goal to give it permanence. Selection of your goals can only be made by you for your own life to give you the power and drive to achieve them.

POINTERS

➤ 1. ALL GOALS HAVE A TIME FACTOR RESTRICTION.

➤ 2. ALL GOALS REQUIRE IDENTIFIABLE ABILITY.

➤ 3. ALL GOALS REQUIRE THE PARTICIPANT'S DRIVE.

➤ 4. ALL GOALS INCLUDE BOTH OPPORTUNITY AND OPPOSITION.

CHAPTER NINE

SOME FALLACIES ABOUT GOAL ORIENTATION

FAMILY

I suppose the most persistent question I am asked about my life is, "How much time do you spend with your family?"

I usually respond with the answer, "Probably more than you do!"

A common fallacy is that a highly goal-orientated person is hard on his family. Yet generally the exact opposite is true. When an individual sets his life program, it includes things he wants to do as well as things he does not want to do.

One of my objectives has always been that I will maintain a strong, close family life, even after the children are married. It is interesting, now that they are all married, that the goal has been maintained and the rewards are indescribable.

Some people find it hard to believe, but I almost never take any work home or discuss my work at home, because that's how I have arranged my goals program. It allows for a close family life. Even in travel I endeavor to keep my time away short and to keep in phone contact regularly. Wherever possible, my wife and I travel together.

To suggest that a person may disadvantage his family by setting a goals program is to display an active ignorance as to what a goals program can do for the one who designs and lives by it. If there is one thing that keeps a marriage harmonious, it is security. And security comes more from planning than by accident. A life goal that includes the responsibilities of family life — for life — is another example of parental and matrimonial love that says in a very meaningful way, "I love you and care for you." When the honeymoon is over, and tensions and disagreements occur, there is nothing more assuring than the knowledge that a plan has been formulated that includes the whole family for mutual support and benefit.

The interesting thing I have found is that even when children grow up and get married and produce grandchildren, the process continues because the family has accepted and appreciated the benefits of life goals. A particular goal in family life can be the arranging of picnics, or barbecues or other occasions that provide opportunities to get together and keep lines of communication open.

In my own family, we purchased a small farm with a cottage and sheep, cattle and horses. So for a number of years, while the children were going through their adolescence, they could expend their boundless energies and release their pent-up frustrations in a positive way by riding horses, repairing fences and driving tractors. The farm also allowed us to live — on weekends — apart from the hustle and bustle of the outside world, and enjoy our evenings together around a big log fire, talking and laughing together. So that I could sleep in a little late on the first morning of a weekend at the farm, we had a simple rule: Nobody made any noise or got up before me, to allow me to replenish my energy. Then I would serve everybody toast and coffee in bed!

A life goal, dare I say, would be of less value without a family goal because of the great gift of family life and the strength attained from it.

POINTERS

➤ 1. **FAMILY GOALS EXPRESS LOVE.**

➤ 2. **FAMILY GOALS GIVE SECURITY.**

➤ 3. **FAMILY GOALS KEEP THE FAMILY TOGETHER.**

COMPASSION

Setting and following a lifelong goals program will necessarily require the exclusion of some things and some people.

Because you set goals which are specific and in time frames, it is impossible to work in other areas. As you set your goals in one direction, you will inevitably bypass other things that could be done and find yourself rejecting proposals and refusing requests. As a result, you may be accused of lacking in compassion or being uncaring. You are not.

The simple fact is that *to fit in to someone else's project will violate your own commitment.*

This is a tough nut to crack and at times a real problem with which to come to grips. You will find you cannot make others see your point of view while they are trying to make you see theirs! But do not think that I am suggesting that your life-goals program should be so tight and inflexible that it is impossible to fit into it anything additional that is enjoyable or worthwhile.

The key to setting and following a successful life-goals program is to allow time to support others.

And at times, of course, there will be the acute emergency requiring immediate attention. You must exercise your own conscience before God on these issues.

Remember, sometimes you only get one chance during a lifetime to help someone in extreme need. To neglect such an opportunity could unsettle you for the rest of your life. But once the crisis is past, it is back to the goals program.

As I have mentioned before, there are some things for which you should be prepared to give up your life goals. But those are rare. In most cases, what seems like a disaster may just be a big hiccup, a postponement in your schedule. (And at times even major events and additional pressure can do wonders for reassessment).

Your life goals must have within their boundaries compassionate causes that make you think and feel beyond yourself. Select compassionate causes carefully and allow for additional time and expertise to be made available.

POINTERS

➤ 1. LIFE GOALS MUST HAVE OPENINGS FOR THE UNEXPECTED.

➤ 2. LIFE GOALS CAN PROGRAM COMPASSIONATE INVOLVE-MENT.

➤ 3. LIFE GOALS PREPARE AND ALLOW YOU TO DO GOOD FOR OTHERS.

SELFISHNESS

It is very easy to focus on life goals with daily affirmations and still be quite selfish. Someone once said that a man can be so busy making a living that he fails to make a life. But it's not necessary to be that way in order to be a goal-setter.

I average about one speaking appointment each week, and in my daily routine I deal with a considerable amount of mail concerning people's problems. I also generally have appointments with individuals each week who are seeking help. At these times I make sure I give as much of myself as possible.

There is no substitute for sharing yourself with others.

In person, you open the door of your heart, which helps you feel as others feel. Financially, of course, you really ought to give, and give generously. But don't wait to hit pay dirt before giving; instead, make it part of your daily existence to be generous.

Many people talk about giving their time, or their expertise, as a proxy for giving money. But there is something quite magical that happens to a person's spirit when he or she can give hard cash continually and consistently throughout life — in good times and in bad.

The giving of cash, expertise, information and, above all, self, is probably the hardest thing to do, and the way in which people rationalize the amount and its frequency is a dynamic illustration of that fact. (If you want to undertake a serious study of this area, read *How To Be Happy Though Rich*).

Goals for life that include giving provide the joy that keeps you going.

POINTERS

➤ 1. **PROGRAM SELFLESS ACTS WHICH INVOLVE YOU PERSONALLY.**

➤ 2. **GIVE WITHOUT TRADING.**

➤ 3. **GIVE CONSISTENTLY.**

CRITICISM

All of us have at one time or another felt the sting of criticism — the injustice of it and the uncertainty of it. Criticism is as sure as death and taxes.

While it will be impossible to avoid criticism, I warn you here and now to expect more of it as you consider goals for life. There are four basic reasons why you can expect to be criticized more in the future. I will list them so that you can be prepared.

You will be criticized because:

1. *You are not conforming to normal behavior.*

Once you set goals for life, with the inherent objectives and obligations, you step away from the crowd; you have broken with conformity.

2. *You possess dreams and purpose which guide and direct your life.*

You will encounter criticism because your life goals are obviously having an effect on you. Your motivation will often be described as arrogance, pride and even ruthlessness. To know where you are going, and how you are going to get there, poses a threat to those who get along by going along.

3. *Your objective planning and motivation mirrors the inadequacy of the critic.*

Most people know they can do better than they are doing. When you confront them with a life that is growing and expanding, it will not go unnoticed, and you will become the object of jealousy and envy.

4. *You have taken control of your own life and have accepted personal accountability for it.*

In taking this course of action, you are suggesting that others do the same. You are challenging and provoking them. By so doing, you will attract their criticism.

POINTERS

➤ 1. **REMEMBER, THE BIGGEST CRITIC GENERALLY DOES THE LEAST WORK.**

118

➤ 2. PAYING ATTENTION TO YOUR CRITICS VALIDATES THEIR CLAIM AND ELEVATES THEM.

➤ 3. IGNORING YOUR CRITICS SAVES TIME AND ENERGY.

➤ 4. NEVER CRITICIZE A CRITIC.

DON'T BE SIDETRACKED

Sometimes your circumstances are suddenly changed, by a recession, bereavement, a crisis or what looks like a great opportunity. Such circumstances, if they get your attention, are generally unusual in content and timing, so be careful about getting sidetracked.

Circumstances that sidetrack you from the main course usually do so in a minor way at first, then, by pseudo-rationalization, you find yourself pursuing that path only to find that you are far from your original objective and have wasted valuable time, energy and money.

There will always crop up special circumstances that seek your attention and which, if pursued, will absorb your energy and thwart your progress. The way to avoid this situation is to have a list of qualifications before you allow circumstances to invade your goals program. There are occasions when new circumstances actually provide an entrance into a goals program because of their proximity to your aims. But be careful and examine anything that comes by unplanned circumstance. Make sure it provides an alternative route to the path you have already prepared.

Enforced goals. While you are scrambling for a foothold so you can stand firm and continue with your goals program, you may have goals actually forced on you. An example could be an increase in interest rates which is far above your budget. Suddenly your cash flow is upset, so you are forced to face an additional, unexpected goal you cannot avoid. How do you handle that kind of situation?

119

The answer is with careful thought and positive action. Your evaluation of the situation should take into consideration the deadlines that must be met. If it is long-term or urgent-term, then a revised goal must be immediately created by formulating a plan, with all the required checkpoints, increasing the size of the goal to meet the demand. Be careful that enforced goals don't knock you off course — keep them in perspective.

Subconscious goals. The subconscious can play tricks with you. Even though you have set a deliberate course of action with all of the qualifications and time frames, every now and then you can sabotage yourself with bad behavior or wrong decisions.

Sometimes you will experience guilt feelings or attitudes because of something you did or didn't do, something you overlooked or did not clear up earlier. At such a time, you need to go back to the first chapter and recheck and reaffirm your value system. Reread Chapter 1 with complete honesty and clarity.

Your subconscious may not be in tune with your conscious thinking. So conflict occurs. What is happening is that your subconscious mind is trying to pursue entirely different goals from those that you have formulated for your life, and this situation must be corrected.

Likewise, examine your subconscious for signals in case you're on the wrong track. The subconscious mind has the facilities of a miraculous filing cabinet and can, in a flash, go over years of experience, picking up thoughts here and there to create an answer or form an opinion on any subject. So treat it with respect.

Tentative goals. Sometimes you may be tempted to set goals tentatively as a means of testing the waters before the big plunge. This should be done infrequently (if ever) because it can become habit forming and can prevent you from using your dream machine for role playing. It may also make you lazy in seeking full and helpful information.

To use a tentative goal indicates uncertainty, and when you are unsure, you will tend to hold back some of your energies and reduce your commitment level. After a while, tentative goals may become a way of life which restricts you and holds you back from greater things.

Life goals cannot be tentative, they must have the sure, firm seal of commitment. Tentative goals are for tentative people and tentative situations. Make sure that they are used in proper context for rare situations.

Ego goals. As I watched a television interview with an executive from a giant corporation which had just crashed, I heard the interviewer ask why a particular incident had caused the collapse of this great industrial empire.

The chief executive responded, rather bravely I thought, "My ego got in the way!"

Ego goals are probably the most dangerous of the sabotaging goals because, as with King Midas, the craving for more and more does nothing to satisfy the appetite.

I have been in the presence of many leaders and listened to their entourage tell them only that which they wanted to hear. This practice distances a leader from the position of leadership to one of "driftsmanship."

Many have fallen or failed to reach their life goals because their ego got in the way and demanded more space until the life goal collapsed for lack of attention.

I am not suggesting that a big ego is wrong, but I am suggesting that an ego out of control is wrong. By being out of control I mean becoming the object of the life goal or pulling down the life goal to gain prominence.

I believe that to be truly successful, a person's total life must be under control. That's why, earlier in this book, I expressed my commitment to the Christian Gospel which elevates Jesus Christ and His principles. I am convinced that in following Him I will be elevated to my highest potential.

POINTERS

> ➤ 1. **DON'T BE SIDETRACKED BY SABOTAGING GOALS.**

> ➤ 2. **DON'T BE SIDETRACKED BY PSEUDO-RATIONALIZATION OF NEW CIRCUMSTANCES.**

> ➤ 3. **DON'T BE SIDETRACKED BY A LUST FOR RECOGNITION.**

CHAPTER TEN

THE GOALS FORMULA

GROUND RULES FOR GOAL-SETTING

Just as there are basic laws relating to physics, there are ground rules for goal-setting. You break these rules at your peril. Keep these laws, and you will succeed. In this chapter, I will outline seven major guidelines for the setting and achieving of goals.

RULE 1: CLEARLY DEFINE YOUR LIFE GOALS IN TERMS OF ULTIMATE ACHIEVEMENT.

Most of the groundwork toward establishing life goals has been covered in previous chapters. It is time now to develop detailed information on your life goals and definitions.

Definitions must include all categories of importance: family life, finances, social life, religion, giving and the support of your country. The world will keep on going without you, but you cannot keep going without involvement in the world. Quite simply, if you become a cold, calculating, single-minded, objective-oriented person without relating to circumstances around you, in the process of reaching your goals, you will isolate yourself from humanity itself.

It may well be that you have cleared away all the superfluous padding already and got down to a concise description of what you are really aiming for. In the previous chapters I have suggested that free flow of thought and the continuance of words with embellishments will help you to stretch your mind and activate your imagination. At this point you must remove the embellishments and tighten your description in an effort to get closer to your precise life goals, both in definition and priority.

Remember, the clearer and more complete your definition, the easier it will be for you to relate to your goals at any moment, and the easier it will be to measure any new opportunity.

To write out your *ultimate life goal* will be difficult because of the enormous commitment level embodied in the overall plan. You are, in fact, trading your unknown future for a confirmed future. While on the surface it appears to be a simple and logical trade, you may find deep down that you would still like the chance to let go and leave it all to circumstance. Your strong resolve at this point must be committed to paper. Your life goal will only become reality as you write it down as a simple, logical statement of faith.

I carry my life goal with me always so I can affirm its charter against anything I do. Because it is enhanced by written clarity, I can, within a moment, evaluate almost any decision against it.

Your ultimate life goal should consist of one thing.

Being one item, it will provide a clear description for all else to conform to it.

My own life goal is confined to just a few lines of writing and, although I have memorized it, I still read it daily for affirmation and motivation.

Once the ultimate life goal is decided and recorded, the next step is to define the *major supportive goals* which thrust that life goal onward to the summit of its achievement. These goals may be numerous, but each will play a major role in the overall plan. Let me illustrate.

I have one ultimate life goal, but I have twenty-nine major secondary goals that support it either directly or indirectly. My goals relating to my family may not directly relate to the total attainment of my life goal, but what a sad day it would be if I reached the summit and lost my greatest asset, which is my family.

There are some major goals relating to books which I want to write, and groups I want to help, which, if not achieved, could be compensated for by increased results in other areas. But, I would still reach my life goal. Other goals are so inter-locked with my ultimate life goal that I must achieve each one in sequence.

The key is the stability of your life goal, in tangible form. Your supportive goals also need clarity and documentation to complete the picture.

The final step in defining your life goal is to define your *minor goals*. These are areas of your life that can be handled with a minimum of fuss. Rarely will a minor goal extend past two years, and if it does, it will be a routine item requiring the input of time rather than concentrated or consistent effort.

The definition of your life goals must now be in the form of a simple written document, expressing in clear terms your ultimate life goal, your major supportive goals — with a clear description of each one — and your minor goals, which support your major goals.

Be prepared to spend prime time completing this task, because you are going to trade your life for it in one form or another.

Go backward and forward over your written description, polishing and pruning where necessary so that the final document paints word pictures of such clarity and purpose that you feel that any change at all would mar the masterpiece.

POINTERS

➤ 1. DESCRIBE IN CLEAR TERMS YOUR ULTIMATE LIFE GOAL.

➤ 2. DESCRIBE YOUR SUBORDINATE MAJOR GOALS.

➤ 3. DESCRIBE YOUR SUBORDINATE MINOR GOALS.

RULE 2: SET OUT YOUR STRATEGY.

It is one thing to set out your life goals in descriptive terms and look at them with satisfaction, but it is something else to set out in clear, detailed terms how you are going to accomplish them. Obviously the ultimate life goal must come first, as it is the overwhelming purpose of your life.

The strategy here is both simple and involved. It is simple because of its definition and its time frame, but involved in its ultimate attainment. I have set my life-goal attainment at eighty-five years of age because I believe this is a reasonable time frame for its realization. This does not limit either my life or my goal — both can be expanded — but for the sake of having something to aim at, I set the goal and its supportive goals to fit into this particular time bracket. I have made allowances in my life goal for expansion should I be blessed with more years than I expect. My life goal is predicated on a measurement of attainment in a specific area of life directly controlled and influenced by my Christian commitment.

My life goal is too personal to declare to others in its entirety, but I share with some selected people its general destiny and course. For my own purpose, I have reduced my life goal into units so that I can measure its progress. This means that I can "strategize" because I can regulate with realistic and uniform measurement.

If you cannot find a measurement to guide your strategy, then you will not know how far you have traveled; and if you don't know how far you have traveled, then you will not know how far you have to go. Without a guide, confusion begins to enter the picture and goals start to lose their sharpness.

With my life goal, I strategize with respect to the educational tools and physical requirements that I need to develop in order to give me the endurance to complete the task. The other requirement is style, which I covered in the earlier chapters. This approach really places an emphasis on quality in the years of attainment.

Having defined your life goal strategy in a general way, it is time to go straight to the bottom of the pile and look at your foundation goals that provide a solid base on which to build. Remember to allocate the most effort to the early years and to foundation building, in order to prevent an unexpected collapse later, because here you are sharpening your skills.

Whatever happens, don't get impatient or despondent because you see little change or response to the outlay of thought and energy. In later years you are going to be just as amazed at the quantum leaps you make with seemingly little or no effort.

Plan every detail of what you need. Determine its purpose and how it fits into your overall plan. The major goals must, of course, fit into the life goal, and yet the substance of the life goal — if it is going to be an effective innovation — must be seen in form and function as you go along. As you work and plan in these areas, you will see a pattern begin to emerge, and each part of the jigsaw enhances the picture.

Your minor goals also must be attended to, fitting into the major goals to create a total life plan. The exercises in the previous chapters have prepared your mind for the planning of your goals. Be sure to mark special milestones or events that emphasize your arrival at particular destinations in your life. If that is impractical, remember the measurement of units and use it to recognize and celebrate each new level of achievement.

POINTERS

> ➤ 1. **STRATEGY CREATES ENERGY.**

> ➤ 2. **STRATEGY SAVES ENERGY.**

> ➤ 3. **STRATEGY GIVES DIRECTION.**

RULE 3: PLAN OUT THE PROBLEMS.

Every long-term plan and every life goal has problem areas which will have to be dealt with. How you react to these problems is going to either increase or decrease the way in which they will be solved. To expect the problems to be solved as you go along is unrealistic. Instead, why not plan for potential problem areas before you commence your life-goals program?

The first problem is always personal and usually has to do with attitudes of belief and commitment. It is at the personal problem level of attitude that the task can become easier if a few simple rules are observed. Problems are always a growth experience. As you tackle the problem areas of your own attitude, and succeed, the greatest and most worthwhile victories are won.

Take another look at yourself and identify the personal areas of dissatisfaction. Place into your goals program, at whatever level you can accept as being correct, a method to root out the problem areas with the personal equipment available.

Most people start out in business or on a goals program undercapitalized, assuming that this is the greatest limiting factor possible. Yet business research and experience have shown that those who start out with huge amounts of capital generally lose it, and in a very short time.

Large capital amounts are not necessary, but large capital plans are. The financial areas of your total life plans need to be attended to probably more than anything else. If you search out the financial problem areas, you will save enormous amounts of time and anguish with respect to your long- and short-term performance. Examine the obstacles that stand in the way of your reaching your life goal, and you will probably see that they will fall into one of three areas.

Problem area number one is personal. These are problems in relation to belief, attitude and self-discipline, and usually are the most difficult to plan out because of the deep thought and harsh investigation required. The earlier chapters regarding a value system will help you to deal with this area.

Problem area number two is financial. Everybody thinks his or her financial problems are in the realm of the "too little" rather than the "too much." Yet a tight budget always teaches resourcefulness and ingenuity, while a more comfortable budget can encourage slothfulness and keep the planner confined in a comfort zone.

Plan your finances carefully and calculate your needs to prevent cash blow-outs, which can collapse your goals structure and bring you back to the starting line with a thud. Do not underestimate the care needed on financial matters, and document your income and your expenditure as a matter of fact, rather than fiction.

Problem area number three is logistical. It may well be that you have decided that you are not in the right place at the right time or that you need to get closer to the action if you are going to reach the apex of your life goal.

I deliberately moved my home from the suburbs to a park setting in the center of the city to save time and body stress. I estimated that I averaged up to eight hours a week traveling to and from my office, which accounts for seven-and-a-half weeks a year sitting behind the wheel of a car! That kind of waste did not equate with my life-goals program of achievement and growth.

Plan your location and movements with respect to your home, place of business, access to national and international flights or whatever your logistical requirements are. Plan out the obstacles that stand in your way.

POINTERS

➤ 1. PROBLEMS CAN BE PLANNED OUT.

➤ 2. THE BIGGEST PROBLEM IS ATTITUDE.

➤ 3. FAILURE TO PLAN IS FAILURE TO MAN.

RULE 4: BUILD IN RESERVES.

There is a great deal of talk today about "burn-out," and many people are forced to rest — even to the point of hospitalization.

What makes an intelligent human being continue to work regardless of the consequences, ignoring mental and physical signals with respect to his or her health?

No army general will continue to drive his men without due regard for their well-being, because the consequence of such an action could very easily give the enemy the edge.

I am not suggesting a coasting along or taking a six-month-vacation twice a year. I am suggesting that you build up intelligent reserves for your body, mind and spirit.

I rarely take any work home because that is my haven from the world. That is where I read, reflect and fortify myself. How else could I go year after year without vacations or rest periods? My method is to get to bed as early as I can, as often as I can, and to obtain stress relief by riding horses or having a massage or a sauna. I try to do those things on a regular basis, so even though I work hard and continuously, I always have reserves.

If you're going to make a mark in life, it is going to be over the long haul, and to do that you are going to have to build in powerful reserves to hedge against unexpected opportunities and reversals. The most important reserves are mental, particularly in the area of self-confidence, affirmations that you are on the right track and total commitment to your life-goals program.

I continually read biographies and autobiographies as encouragement to my own spirit. By reading of the experiences of others, with their victories and their misadventures, I can build my confidence reserves, which are ever ready in case of a calamity or an unusual opportunity.

The other area where reserves are required is in dealing with people, and those human resource reserves must be planned. During difficult periods in your life, when you have your back to the wall, and information or help is required, very often it is not *what* you know but *who* you know that counts.

Build into your life goals *people reserves* in different areas of concern and need. Obviously, this means planning and selectivity with mutual respect. In so doing, your own life as well as your life goals will be protected by a kind of insurance policy of people in case of trouble.

It is amazing to me the number of people who call me only when they need help, and usually at the most inappropriate times. They know in some way that because of my Christian call I must respond. Yet I would have to be less than honest if I did not say that I wish they would call me occasionally just as a greeting to balance the budget!

Build in people reserves as your greatest barrier against difficult situations, and always try to be in the front line offering others help. It is truly more blessed to give than to receive.

I have a few words in my goals program that read: "I will always keep sensible cash reserves." I strive to have a benchmark of fluid financial reserves to protect my family and my life-goals program against the unexpected events of this life.

Just imagine, if you will, that you are ten years down the road toward your life goal, and a recession hits your business or even your country. How then will a life-goals program be continued without some financial reserves?

I have noticed with unhappy regularity the number of organizations that collapse because they lack strong financial reserves. Yet it seems inevitable from time to time that businesses, industry and government experience recession. Those who survive it are bigger, better and stronger, while those who are not prepared for it either close or reduce in size and lose their effectiveness.

Take care to ensure that your financial assets are solid and not the type that can be worth a fortune one day and worthless the next. Also make sure that your assets are inflation-proof and will minimize taxation requirements; otherwise, at your hour of need your resources may be restricted.

In preparing your simple life-goals formula, build in reserves, not to provide a comfort zone of complacency, but rather as a battle zone for survival enabling you to continue and stretch your real life goal.

POINTERS

➤ 1. MENTAL, PHYSICAL AND SPIRITUAL RESERVES ARE GOOD SENSE.

➤ 2. PEOPLE IN KEY POSITIONS ARE STRONG RESERVES.

➤ 3. FINANCIALLY FLUID ASSETS ARE NECESSARY PROTECTIVE RESERVES.

RULE 5: RELATE EVERYTHING TO A TIME FRAME.

Often I am amused by people who say they are determined to do something and then fail to put the target of their determination into a time frame. The very word "determination" embodies the word "termination," which expresses the full meaning of the word. All your dreams, desires, ideals and goals are but a vapor without the strong, firm, searching eyes of finalization.

Everything that you have stressed inwardly or on paper during your progress through this book needs to be examined against and within a definite, limited time frame.

If you are contemplating some grand scheme for your life (and I hope you are), then such a plan must focus itself upon your life goal within a reasonable life span. Should your plan not reasonably fit into the balance of your life, then it must be altered to conform.

I am not for one moment suggesting a reduction of your life plan, but rather a revision and examination to allow for more to be done in less time. Now is the time to examine in detail, and within practical terms, your additional educational requirements, to allow if need be, a time frame for study and examination. It may pay to do several things at once if you are faced with institutionalized time frames; otherwise, the progress in that area could drag behind the progress in other areas which will unnecessarily limit you.

Evaluate time frames and allow for planning because new information, and changes in world and local events, may add different measurements of pressure in different directions. The life-goals program must be laid out carefully against your major and minor goals, individually assessed with careful, informative feedback for completion and then programmed into the overall plan. This programming must allow for delays or early achievement, with alternatives, so no time will be wasted by either of these possible eventualities.

Some of your goals may only commence when others are finished. Then other requirements may have to be slotted in, while others may have to be phased out. The life goal is immovable. The other goals are the tools to support the attainment of the ultimate objective. Relate to time frames so that both highly pressured and less pressured goals are patterned. This enables an allocation of energy.

Remember, we are talking of a long haul and, while it is important to expend much effort launching the program, a continuity of pressure will result in fuzzy thinking and treadmill activity.

Consider also the completion of a part of your total program, and document its occurrence along with what your thoughts and responses are. This will give you encouragement to press on. Remember that the end of each goal becomes the beginning of another. After a while each new beginning will seem to require less energy because your success ratio will improve, and you will better understand the process.

Take some time to write down each goal on a piece of paper and spread each goal out on a desk over a time frame map representing your life. Then move each one around until the pattern is completed to your satisfaction.

At the risk of repeating myself too much, I have to emphasize again that ample time must be given to the demands of change. Be aware that a change does not represent an opportunity just to avoid pressure or commitment.

I went broke three times over a five-year period, stayed in substandard hotels and drove sometimes for days on hot, dusty, unimproved roads. But rather than getting closer to my tangible goals, I was becoming farther removed from them! However, during that period I was being equipped mentally and spiritually for a huge quantum leap that only became available because of my disappointments in the past. What really happened was that I became a different person during those five years, and the experiences and knowledge that I gained during that difficult period prepared me well to recognize a good opportunity when I saw one and gave me the ability to handle it once I took advantage of it.

POINTERS

➤ 1. **EXPRESS EACH GOAL IN A TIME FRAME.**

➤ 2. **MIX SUITABLE GOALS IN THE SAME TIME FRAME.**

➤ 3. **FIT ALL GOALS INTO TIME FRAMES.**

The Goals Formula

Rule 1: *Clearly define your goals.*

Rule 2: *Set out your strategy.*

Rule 3: *Plan out the problems.*

Rule 4: *Build in reserves.*

Rule 5: *Relate everything to a time frame.*

Rule 6: *Create a master plan.*

Rule 7: *"Actionize" your plan now.*

Rule 6: Create a Master Plan.

Now is the time for the finale in respect to setting and solidifying your life goals and their supportive structures. You have separately dealt with each area in the goal-setting segments of the Goals Formula, and now all of these must be welded into a master plan for the achievement of those goals.

You may have considered covering each of the areas in the Goals Formula on a different-colored sheet of paper and putting them in a folder for easy access with indexed subjects. This one — number six — is the ultimate master plan and should be made distinctive by way of its layout.

There also must be space allowed to write in comments and progress with starting and completion dates included. All goals, strategy, problems, reserves and time frames must now be made to mesh and harmonize with each other. The foundation stones which represent your commencement goals must dovetail with supportive goals and the ultimate life goal to complete the picture. The strategies must mix and match so that no goal is in conflict with another, causing a waste of energy.

Try to work out areas of common ground in your strategy which, for very little extra effort, could double or triple the results simply by mixing the components.

Collectively summarize the cost of your master plan in the areas of time, money and personal freedom as well as in the less tangible areas of life, and build a word picture of such a cost. Now harmonize that cost in time frames.

It will be necessary to protect your progress by including in your master plan checkpoints for attainment and other scores that need to be reached before moving on. Discipline will be necessary to prevent moving ahead on a more enjoyable part of your plan before catching up with other areas that may not be as fulfilling. Also, make sure that your financial and other reserves are in place. Don't even move without that point being clear.

The longer you progress in your life-goals program, the more you have to lose. I am amazed at the high risks some people take just to be able to say, "I got there early." Keep your reserves for setbacks; don't use them for a leap forward in case of an unexpected emergency.

This part of your life-goals planning is probably the hardest because it requires you to think again through every area of your plans and redream your dreams, enabling them to be put into workable plans related to hard facts, time frames and financial and normal human restraints.

Do not forget the lessons of the earlier chapters on achievement, and particularly the biblical charge, "As a man thinks in his heart, so is he!" From this Scripture begin to get the picture, from God's point of view, that you literally become what you think about. Psychological and behavioral science also confirms that fact.

Whatever you do, don't flush out with facts the dream areas of your life goals, or limit in any way your ability to grow and to achieve. Rather, put them in harmony with the five main areas of the Goals Formula. Do not limit their impact or scope, but place them in a framework that will give opportunity for the unexpected breakthrough, and, at the same time, protect you against the harshness and destruction of an unexpected difficulty or catastrophe.

What you are doing is summarizing all the loose ends and blending them together to form a predictable plan for your life.

Days, weeks and even months spent on clarification of this plan will not only save you years of work, but also much pain. Remember, the plan does not do the work for you! You do that yourself!

What the plan does is point the way and identify the tools. It is up to you to provide the motivation, the wisdom and the "stickability" in getting there.

POINTERS

➤ 1. **SUMMARIZE THE FORMULA.**

➤ 2. **HARMONIZE ALL PLANS.**

➤ 3. **PROTECT YOUR PROGRESS WITH CHECKPOINTS.**

RULE 7: "ACTIONIZE" YOUR PLAN NOW.

No great achievement can be realized without action, and so it is with goal-setting.

Theories are great. Knowledge can be power. Good intentions are only weak promises. But decisive action can turn the smallest dream into a magnificent reality.

So "actionize" your goal promptly and provoke it by action continually. In so doing, you will fulfill your life goal.

CHAPTER ELEVEN

HOW TO MAINTAIN YOUR GOALS

PAY ATTENTION TO DETAIL

As I move from city to city and country to country, I am forever on the lookout for ideas and differences. In particular I notice the areas in which men and women excel as separate groups — which, in my opinion, proves again that the differences between the sexes are more than biological.

On one occasion I was making inquiries in a travel organization when I noticed that all the staff in the office were women. I said to the senior female executive, "I know why there are no men in this office."

"Why?" she asked.

"You have women here because they can handle repetitive work and pay attention to detail," I replied.

She agreed.

The hardest job I have found in all business life is to get men to pay attention to detail. On the other hand, one of my other great difficulties is getting women to stop majoring on minor issues.

It seems to me that to get a combination of the best of both sexes — that is, to get women to see the big picture and to get men to handle detail — is very difficult, although not impossible. When there is a combination of both characteristics in one individual, the result is a powerful, persuasive and capable person. I believe that the skill of seeing the full picture can be acquired just as attention to detail can be acquired.

I remember well the frustration my son, Peter, caused in our office during his early years because he would not complete details and follow up documentation of sales. The situation became so bad that I very nearly lost my best female senior executive over it. Today Peter is a complete professional, and I doubt whether it would be possible for anyone to handle detail any better than he. The thing that caused the change was a simple law:

If you don't inspect, you cannot expect.

Peter found himself constantly chasing down old sales and patching up what he thought was completed work, so he changed his attitude and approach. In other words, he found it more profitable financially and more peaceful emotionally, to finish each job to the last detail. He learned to ask questions and seek out information before, during and after the sale to ensure that it all proceeded with a minimum of fuss. The results were remarkable. His new habits have expressed themselves in returns in many different ways.

At times you must ask the seemingly silly question and sometimes seek out more information than you need so you won't find yourself caught in a jam. I'm not suggesting that you become paranoid, but you will need to check, double-check and sometimes check again. Also you may need to get people to repeat instructions to make sure they understand.

Some years ago I was faced with a situation in my business in which I could not get clients to respond to our correspondence. As is the custom in my organization, from time to time I read outgoing correspondence. Suddenly I saw the problem. I met with our office staff and asked one employee if she could give me a time frame for the phrase "as soon as possible."

"Well," she said, "it really depends on the person's circumstances and the urgency factor that they see in the request."

I then asked another staff member to respond to the question, "Could you contact this office at your earliest convenience?"

Again I received a response that was quite ambiguous.

I then asked another staff member to respond to the request, "Could you contact our office urgently?"

He said that it meant that he would expect a response within a week or so.

I'm sure you can see what I'm getting at. I changed that situation by getting all staff to send out correspondence with a specific date for an expected reply and a diary entry for immediate follow-up if no reply was forthcoming. The result was startling because people respond to clear instruction and advice.

The amount of work created by a mistake usually requires four times the amount of time required to do it right.

I saw an unforgettable cartoon on the wall of an executive suite. The caption said it all: "Measure twice and saw once." Good advice! Attention to detail will put you light-years ahead of others, and if you make the same mistake twice, remember it so it will never happen again.

POINTERS

➤ 1. **ATTENTION TO DETAIL CAN BE LEARNED.**

➤ 2. **INSPECT WHAT YOU EXPECT.**

➤ 3. **WHEN YOU MAKE THE SAME MISTAKE TWICE, REMEMBER IT.**

MAKE DAILY AFFIRMATIONS

Keeping track of life goals requires diligence and perseverance. Concentration can easily be fragmented and the problems of life that beset all of us from time to time can seem overwhelming. Before you know where you are, your goals are forgotten and your dreams smashed.

I have found that daily, weekly and monthly affirmations keep me on the track and provide, in a very real way, motivation and growth. I have, in written form, my life goal in detail with my twenty-nine major goals in chronological order with supportive helps and minor goals up until my eighty-fifth birthday. To have that information in written form is in itself something of a success in planning. But what if I put it under lock and key and only returned to it on my eighty-fifth birthday for evaluation? Do you think I would be able to arrive on time and keep that which I have committed?

I read my life goal every morning and confirm my major goals every week. I write a letter to myself every month explaining where I am in relation to my goals. The interesting thing here is that I then have a look at the letter I wrote to myself twelve or fifteen months ago and compare it with what has happened since. I then find out where I have lied!

My experience is that unless I keep short accounts with myself in respect to affirmation and progress, I falter and start to make excuses. Then my self-esteem suffers because I lose my integrity.

I measure every single day, scoring twenty-five points for simplicity, twenty-five points for desperation, twenty-five points for planning and twenty-five points for daily achievements. This way I can keep close watch on my standard of performance. (For more detailed information on daily assessment, read my book *How To Be Happy Though Rich*.)

Here's a helpful hint: Keep loose leaves or extra pages in your goals book to allow for the addition of quick ideas you can enter from time to time that will enhance your program.

I believe this technique of writing in a book everything I have done well in life gives me the added boost I need when faced with a large challenge or a difficult situation. The Bible does say in the book of Philippians, "Whatever things are true, noble, right, pure, lovely and admirable, think of these things." (Phil. 4:8 NIV, paraphrased).

I am very conscious of the negativism surrounding us all, and of the desperate need to repel that influence with positive affirmation. So I am suggesting that you write down all the things you do well and read over them on those occasions when you feel that negativism is creeping in.

Another simple thing I do to remind myself of my goals is to carry a small card with a reduced photograph on it of everything that must be done for the next ten years. I keep this card in my pocket for easy reference to check progress and evaluate anything suggested to me. In this way I ensure that it fits in with my life-goal plans.

Affirming yourself also involves mixing with people who are achievers and always looking for the individual who can do something better than you, so that you can learn from that person. Good books continually appear on the market with descriptions of new techniques and interesting stories of how other people either did great things or developed theories of suggested ways things can be done. Avoid those people who are forever complaining and pouring out negative thoughts. I have found that it takes a great deal more positive input to overcome negative input. It is almost as if you have to stand sentinel at the gate of your mind and challenge thoughts as they come to you for negative or positive charge!

Try to spend one hour a week going over your goals program, measuring performance and planning the next move. The more time you spend affirming your goals, the more they become a part of you. But do not substitute paper action for proper action or activity for objectivity.

POINTERS

➤ 1. **AFFIRM YOUR GOAL DAILY.**

➤ 2. **KEEP A TEN-YEAR GOAL CARD IN YOUR WALLET OR PURSE.**

➤ 3. **CREATE A BOOK ON THINGS YOU HAVE DONE WELL.**

EXPAND AS YOU GO

As the clouds of limitation lift and new horizons of growth present a wider picture, then is the time to expand your goals. None of us, however much we may dream or project, can accurately predict our final growth rate. The bondage of past and present restraints crowd our thoughts, and our thoughts in turn provide our goals. So we must have goals that are expandable in kind and in direction.

For instance, it may be that your ultimate life goal is to develop the biggest and most successful business of its kind in your city. As your knowledge and experience grow and the years unfold, you may find that your earlier life goal has expanded. It now may be to have the largest business of its kind in the state or the nation. The focus must be on the direction you are going. The moment you lose sight of that direction, problems arise.

A business in our city expanded and grew, manufacturing and distributing electrical hardware items for other manufacturing companies and retail outlets. Over the years this particular company concentrated more in a particular direction until it reached the stage of limited specialization. The end of that company came when it tried to keep the organization going although its specialized goods were no longer required. What had happened was it had worked itself into a limited market with limited items, so that its whole business stood or fell on one product.

Do not limit your goals in a direction that has an abrupt end.

Rather choose a direction that can include, absorb and benefit by change.

Never let your life goal be changed or dictated by the major or minor goals — they are there to serve the life goal, not to set or change direction. It could be that the major or minor goals expand or take a different direction over a period of time. You may even create new ones and drop some, but it is all in the purpose of serving the ultimate life goal, to give it the nurture and support it needs.

POINTERS

➤ 1. AS YOUR LIMITATIONS LIFT, SO LIFT YOUR GOALS.

➤ 2. BE DIRECTION-ORIENTATED.

➤ 3. DON'T LET MAJOR OR MINOR GOALS RESET DIRECTION.

CHANGE YOUR LIFESTYLE

As you grow and expand toward your life goal, your personality will change. It is not that you will become a different person, but rather a better person because you will be becoming more fulfilled. Sometimes it is hard to imagine that the change will take place, but the inevitable will occur, and you will go where once you did not want to go. So you will become involved in different social and political areas.

The car you drive may be upgraded, and the home in which you live may change or expand because your standard of living is improved. Because you have increased your earnings, so you are able to enjoy some material benefits. A changed lifestyle definitely changes you, even if only in what you say and where and how you say it.

You will have influence, and what you say can and will influence other people. So you will become news, and you may even be sought out for public comment. Even your vacations may take on a new and exciting meaning.

No one can take away from us the memories of the wonderful times we had many years ago with our children camping on the beach. The fun we shared together in those days will never be forgotten. But today, with the family grown up, our vacations might be anywhere in the world. Our lifestyle has changed, and so will yours.

Your friends will change, not I hope, because you think you are now too sophisticated and elevated to retain old friendships, but because some will leave you over a period of time. Because of your growth and gradual change in lifestyle, some of your old friends will be unable to accept the change. But the fact is that they will simply no longer feel comfortable with you, and you will have to come to grips with that situation.

Do not stunt your lifestyle by putting limitations on its growth, but maintain good manners and a respect for the individuality of others. Avoid flaunting your wealth, particularly with those less fortunate. Some friends, of course, will grow with you, and others, who really love you, will stay and enjoy with you the new lifestyle and encourage you to push on. They may even be a little proud of what their dear friend has achieved!

As your lifestyle changes, be outgoing and develop poise and etiquette for every occasion. If you are not quite sure how to handle yourself in your new social environment, set a minor goal to study the subject by reading books and observing what others do. It takes a certain amount of skill to entertain people graciously and to make everyone feel welcome, wanted and comfortable. But a few well-selected comments or questions can usually make even the most reserved and timid person feel at ease. Don't feel guilty or uncomfortable about your new-found lifestyle, but rather be grateful for goals accomplished and access to more opportunities.

I find it disconcerting to see seemingly good, honest Christians who have attained a degree of wealth, attempt to portray a poverty-stricken lifestyle — refusing to talk about money and, in some respects, practicing deceit to prevent demands being made upon them.

You should always be mindful of the fact that your growth and lifestyle will act as a model for others. It will also act as a point of judgment on your character and personality. Make an effort to be complimentary and uplifting with others, and you will be welcome wherever you go.

POINTERS

➤ 1. **EXPAND YOUR LIFESTYLE GRACIOUSLY.**

➤ 2. **MAKE OTHERS FEEL COMFORTABLE WHEN THEY ARE AROUND YOU.**

➤ 3. **DO NOT FEEL GUILTY ABOUT CHANGE.**

REAFFIRM YOUR CHARTER

There will come times during your journey toward your life goal that you will put on the brakes and question the wisdom of it all, asking yourself: What am I doing here? Where am I going? Am I on the right track? These times of self-doubt occur as you bump into life's rough edges, or have sand kicked in your face once too often. Don't be discouraged or upset; I often ask myself these same questions.

This is the time to reflect quickly on past achievements. Remind yourself that the victories you have attained have come about because you accepted you life-goals charter and pushed on regardless of the consequences.

As you complete certain milestones in your life, you will rise above your old self and expand what you thought were limiting factors. It is good to reaffirm your goals. Reaffirming your charter is necessary because you are probably now in a comfort zone, and having endured some pain to reach that zone, reaffirmation is required to endure more and complete the course.

What a sad picture we would be if we reached a comfort zone somewhere on the way to a life goal and dwelt there too long, only to find toward the end of life that we had failed to complete the course. Having failed because of unwillingness is something quite different.

In reaffirming your charter, it is wise to investigate new advances in technology and new techniques that will give new life to old ideas, particularly, and more often, after you pass the halfway mark. The temptation to wander will be strong at that point. The easiest way to find out whether you are starting to slip into a rut is to observe how often you talk about what you have done in the past rather than what more you are going to do in the future. In other words, you need a futuristic outlook, to stay on the track.

If you find you are losing your hunger to grow and your charter has lost its bloom, then move into younger company where people are still pursuing and growing. Avoid older company where discussions are on the past. It could be that the halfway mark of your life goal is the most dangerous place to be and at that point you need to refine them. Get alone again and study your target areas and embellish and improve some of the major goals.

By now you have learned many lessons and gained insight into your own capabilities, so on the basis of where you have come from, you have a good idea of how much farther you can go. Do not slacken or be seduced into involvement in some side issue.

On moving away from your charter you lose an appreciation for the business climate and associated events. Sometimes it is almost impossible to recapture lost ground.

POINTERS

➤ 1. IT IS HUMAN TO QUESTION WHAT YOU ARE DOING HERE.

➤ 2. BE FUTURISTIC IN YOUR CONVERSATION AND OUTLOOK.

➤ 3. ASSOCIATE WITH YOUNG-THINKING, AGGRESSIVE PEOPLE.

MAKE A QUANTUM LEAP

As you progress toward and achieve your major and minor goals and approach the object of your life goal, you need to reassess your assets in relation to the task left. Earlier, your ideals were obvious and your finances were restricted, but closer to the top life can become routine and you may lose that special feeling that makes you stretch and strive. In losing that edge, you are putting restrictions on the best years of your life and hindering the fulfillment of your greatest potential.

Life at the top can have many distractions, and it is when you are popular and in demand that you may confuse activity with objectivity. What a waste to let all of that ability continue at cruising speed when the engines are just broken-in and ready for the race of a lifetime.

In the previous section, I suggested that it was necessary to stay on the track, but now I am encouraging you to take a quantum leap on that track. The reason I suggest such a bold move is that it will release all of that pent-up power into a constructive force that will realize the maximum amount of remaining potential.

A quantum leap could mean a doubling of your life goal or an increased emphasis on major goals — even an expansion of all remaining goals under new planning and strategy, but this time within tight time frames.

A quantum leap means just what it says: a big move forward. If you want some kind of guideline, you will need to make it large enough to get your conscious and sub-conscious attention and make you just a little bit scared so your total thinking process will be activated.

A quantum leap does not mean gambling what you have achieved for double or nothing. Rather, it means retaining what you have and securing it. Then, with new vigor and vision, you launch into an explosion of growth equal to but not beneath your abilities or outside of your time frames. It is now time to move into

149

new directions of thought and energy that will act as a benchmark for others to follow.

But best of all, now is the time for you to be at your best, performing now more than ever in total harmony with your body, mind and spirit. You will probably find it will prolong your life, and you will be happier with your work than you have been before.

POINTERS

➤ 1. **A QUANTUM LEAP CREATES ENERGY.**

➤ 2. **A QUANTUM LEAP USES ALL POTENTIAL.**

➤ 3. **A QUANTUM LEAP IS NOT A GAMBLE.**

TREAT OTHER PEOPLE WITH DIGNITY

I was in a foreign country as a guest of the government, and we were inspecting some irrigation schemes to assist the local residents in growing crops. I asked my driver to stop and went into the fields to speak to a woman working with a hand hoe.

When I spoke to her, she responded by calling me "master." I don't think I have ever been as shocked as I was at that moment, and to this day I still feel the indignity that one human should be addressed that way by another. As I moved throughout that country I made sure that I never allowed anyone to call me that again, and that I did my best to relate to everyone I met on an equal basis.

Well do I remember as a child some people who lived in a big house behind us who were to be treated as something more than human. We should remember that we all depart from this earth equal. I hear a lot of talk about being a good loser, but very little is said about being a good winner. To be a good winner is to treat people with dignity, respecting the right to proper courtesy and concern for others whoever they are.

Many times in my life I have experienced help or encouragement from small courtesies, well in excess of that which I had given and at the most crucial time.

Respecting others, in particular those who are not as well off as you, may be an encouragement to them to strive and better themselves. However, great care should be taken not to be condescending or artificial. Giving dignity to others gives dignity to yourself.

REAFFIRM YOUR FORMULA TO OTHERS

As you progress and work on your life goal, it will become quite obvious to everyone that you have a formula that works. Give your formula to others so they in turn may grow.

I have friends who continually send me new books, cassette tapes and magazine clippings of things that they have found helpful, and in doing so they have doubled or tripled the value of their find.

As you move through life, set aside good ideas and give them to others to encourage and inspire them.

If you find someone who has gone broke or is having difficulties, share with that person your own story of the difficult moments you faced and tell him or her about the formula you used in solving the problem.

As you share your goals with others, you reaffirm your own goals and gain additional emphasis and encouragement. Holding tight-fistedly to your newly discovered plans and formulae to create growth and solve problems restricts you and everyone else.

GIVE GOD THE GLORY

As a Christian, I believe that we humans were created by God for His glory, and we remain here on this earth because of His goodness.

I believe that we are lost until we accept Jesus Christ as our personal Savior and the Lord of our lives. At that point, we come under God's grace and receive the gift of everlasting life.

I further believe that our sojourn on this earth is full of opportunity to serve and to live out our convictions and participate in the joy of belonging to God through faith in His Son, Jesus Christ.

Any foolishness in this book I accept as my own, and for any wisdom included I give God the glory.

WHAT IS YOUR DECISION?

If you have never received Jesus Christ as your personal Lord and Savior, why not do it right now? Simply repeat this prayer with sincerity: "Lord Jesus, I believe that You are the Son of God. I believe that You became man and died on the cross for my sins. I believe that God raised you from the dead and made You the Savior of the world. I confess that I am a sinner and I ask You to forgive me, and to cleanse me of all my sins. I accept Your forgiveness, and I receive You as my Lord and Savior. In Jesus' name, I pray. Amen."

"...if you confess with your mouth, 'Jesus is Lord,' and believe in your heart that God raised him from the dead, you will be saved. For it is with your heart that you believe and are justified, and it is with your mouth that you confess and are saved....for, 'Everyone who calls on the name of the Lord will be saved.'"

Romans 10:9,10,13 NIV

"If we confess our sins, he is faithful and just and will forgive us our sins and purify us from all unrighteousness."

1 John 1:9 NIV

Now that you have accepted Jesus as your Savior:

1. Read your Bible *daily* — it is your spiritual food that will make you a strong Christian.

2. Pray and talk to God *daily* — He desires for the two of you to communicate and share your lives with each other.

3. Share your faith with others. Be bold to let others know that Jesus loves them.

4. Regularly attend a local church where Jesus is preached, where you can serve Him and where you can fellowship with other believers.

5. Let His love in your heart touch the lives of others by your good works done in His name.

Please let us know of the decision you made. Write:

Honor Books
P.O. 55388
Tulsa, OK 74155

Peter J. Daniels came from a disadvantaged background and his early years were plagued with illiteracy and ignorance, yet he built a large business in real estate and serves on international boards extending to the four corners of the earth.

For a third of a century he has successfully studied, absorbed and experienced first hand the elusive field

of business and at times worked with some of the most dynamic corporate and intellectual giants of this century.

He has a no-debt philosophy, is personally wealthy and readily adjusts to any situation. His keen intellect, experience and sharp mind produces simple, effective answers to complex problems with a commitment to the free enterprise system within benevolent boundaries and under strong principles. He is an international author of substance and quantity and one of the world's highest paid public speakers.

His network of contacts throughout the world has been the result of a twenty-year involvement which incurs as many as two hundred air flights annually to fulfil schedules and endeavors to meet any genuine need.

**To contact the author,
address all correspondence to:**

Peter J. Daniels
World Centre for Entrepreneurial Studies
38-40 Carrington Street
Adelaide, South Australia 5000
AUSTRALIA
Tel: (08) 231-0111 Fax: (08) 211-8423

Other Titles by Peter J. Daniels

Books

How To Be Happy Though Rich

How To Handle a Major Crisis

How To Be Motivated All the Time

How To Have the Awesome Power of Public Speaking

Miss Phillips You Were Wrong!

Tutorial Programs

Destiny

*How To Get More Done
and Have Time Left Over*

*How To Create Your Own Dynamic
Mission Statement That Works*

Additional copies of this book available
at your local bookstore.

Tulsa, Oklahoma